Why God?

Why God?

Jim Thompson

Bishop of Bath and Wells

MOWBRAY

Mowbray
A Cassell imprint
Wellington House, 125 Strand, London WC2R 0BB
PO Box 605, Herndon, VA 20172

© Jim Thompson 1997

First published 1997

British Library Cataloguing-in-Publication Data
A catalogue for this book is available from the British Library.

ISBN 0 264 67388 3

Cover photograph: Ann Cook, Glastonbury

Typeset by BookEns Limited, Royston, Herts
Printed and bound in Great Britain by Biddles Ltd,
Guildford and King's Lynn

Contents

References to the Bible are usually to book, chapter and verse: 1 Corinthians 13.4 is the First Letter (or Epistle) to the Corinthians, chapter 13, verse 4. Psalm references are to Psalm number and verse.

For a complete listing of the books of the Bible, see adjacent page.

THE BOOKS OF THE OLD TESTAMENT

Genesis
Exodus
Leviticus
Numbers
Deuteronomy
Joshua
Judges
Ruth
1 Samuel
2 Samuel
1 Kings
2 Kings
1 Chronicles
2 Chronicles
Ezra
Nehemiah
Esther
Job
Psalms
Proverbs

Ecclesiastes
Song of Songs
Isaiah
Jeremiah
Lamentations
Ezekiel
Daniel
Hosea
Joel
Amos
Obadiah
Jonah
Micah
Nahum
Habakkuk
Zephaniah
Haggai
Zechariah
Malachi

THE BOOKS OF THE NEW TESTAMENT

Matthew
Mark
Luke
John
Acts
Romans
1 Corinthians
2 Corinthians
Galatians
Ephesians
Philippians
Colossians
1 Thessalonians
2 Thessalonians

1 Timothy
2 Timothy
Titus
Philemon
Hebrews
James
1 Peter
2 Peter
1 John
2 John
3 John
Jude
Revelation

To Ben and Anna

Introduction –
A personal note

The greatest day of my life was the day I discovered that God loved me – not only that he existed but that he *loved* me. That discovery came after a long search and a time of arguing quite fiercely against faith. The discovery began a change, both of my own identity and also of the way I looked at that identity. It gave me the courage to be myself. It gave me the freedom and sense of purpose I had been looking for. Because of what that love did for me, it made me look at other people in a totally different way. Ever since that discovery of God I have been trying to communicate him. This is not a desire to bully people into a mould, but to see them discover abundant life. Once you have been blessed by the love of God, it's very hard to keep quiet about it. So I'm still rattling on some 30 years after the event.

In one sense this story begins at home. As Christian parents, my wife, Sally, and I have brought up two children who are now in their twenties. They are, to our eyes, lovely people and our most precious friends. They are confident and independent people who have not as yet found God. They have their own thoughtful and authentic ethics, but do not have worship and prayer to nourish, judge or inform them. They are very loving and alive, but do not overtly build their life and love on God. They accept and love us, and can see how important our faith in God is to us, but do not feel at the moment they need God to lead the good life. Many young people see in older generations a failure to live up to religious and moral claims, and find a lack of joy in those who say their joy is God.

Why God?

I want to write a letter to cross the generation gap – to write it out of loving and longing. I hope it may be of some use to those who travel the same way. It is written in particular for those who want to have the faith explained and want to think it through, without somehow switching off their own experience and wasting their God-given minds. When God finally got through to me, I wanted to explore the faith, to search it and try it out within my own world. A kindly Presbyterian minister gave me a book by J. B. Phillips called *Your God is Too Small*. It is still a great book, but so much has changed since then. We are searching for God in a strange land. I hope this may be the sort of book which I could hand to my own children and to any searcher for God – young or old – in our own day. I hope and pray that it will assist them in thinking out what they believe.

My thanks are due to all those who have challenged and nourished me in the journey and especially to Ruth who encouraged me to write the book, to Ben and Anna, our children, Julian, Patrick and Professor Romaine Hervey who read the script, to my chaplain Canon Mark Wright who read the proofs, and to Penny Ritchie who typed it in all its versions. It could not have been written if my colleagues had not granted me a sabbatical and my wife Sally had been intolerant of my getting out of bed at 5.00 am to write before the heatwave burnt all thoughts from my head.

One

Discovering God today

I was having supper with some friends: parents from my generation and their actor son. We were discussing the title of this book. The mother and father said the title should not include the word 'God' because it would be a big turn-off for the very people who I hoped would read it. Their son said – and I don't think he said it just for the sake of argument – that the title must include 'God' because that is what it is about and for many of his generation God is an open question. Perhaps my generation are too aware of the barriers to belief in God and not sufficiently aware of the spiritual search going on today because, on the surface, the young generation looks so different to ours.

I enjoy the hit comedy *Absolutely Fabulous* because it turns the generation stereotypes upside-down: the mother behaves like an adolescent and the daughter is the only responsible person in sight. They do not communicate, however, and both are unhappy in their extremes.

I have been taught a great deal by my own children and their friends. I admire their loyalty and love for each other, their honesty and their mutual support. I relish their sense of fun and capacity for enjoyment. I'm envious of their lack of inhibition about sexuality, but sometimes wish it was more firmly rooted in fidelity. Although I admire their freedom in personal relationships, I can see it also brings pain and loss through broken partnerships. I cherish the way that their own moral views have emerged and developed. I rejoice in their colour blindness with people and their sense of racial justice. I envy their sense of adventure. I also believe that they have many difficulties to face which were never even an option for me: job insecurity and even long-term unemployment with its sense of failure and rejection; the ideas of the good life pumped out at them day by day in the media; and the real lack of vision in our society. So many have also experienced the bitterness of their parents' break-up and its effects. It is to them and their generation in particular that these thoughts are offered. I hope it may also be of use to my generation for our spiritual journey as well as for dialogue with our adult children.

The younger generation often rightly question the legacy they have inherited. Although some of them were caught up for a time in the yuppie phenomenon, many others were not and have found it depressing to see the way in which our values have been so determined by money and materialism, where so much is left to the market – their health care, their education, their job opportunities. They are inheriting a society in which many people are faced with unemployment affecting every level of skill and class. They have also inherited a spiritual vacuum and a devastating lack of confidence in politicians, both at local and national level. This discourages commitment and participation. It stimulates a detached and cynical humour and gives every excuse for retreating into personal and private agenda with little sense of community. Perhaps the final proof of this vacuum has been the financial and psychological investment in the National Lottery, in which we gamble money (£128 million in one day) which could transform the lives of so many millions of people who are starving, wounded in war, homeless or just deprived. Its vice is already showing in signs of the addiction and unhappiness caused by such false dreams and it is a pervasive demonstration of an emptiness in the spirit of the age which my generation have handed on to the next. We have even corrupted charity by greed.

The church too can be a barrier to discovering God, but I believe it is being renewed and wrestling with important issues. In its *Faith in the City* report and all the work that followed it, the church faced up to the problems in the inner cities and the big housing estates and even shifted political policy by the learning process. In spite of division, we now have the ordination of women and have struggled with many gender questions which society has not yet solved. We are also part of a world-wide movement whose greatest growth and challenge is to be found in the African continent. I make this point because I feel that the stuffy image of the church is a big block. It is in and through the church that we have to follow up any discovery we make of God. It so often happens that a person is stimulated to think about God, but cannot find the person or the community with whom to explore it further. I increasingly believe that there are churches where the seeker can find encouragement and listening ears.

But the greater problem is that in our age there are many people for whom God has become so small as to be all but non-existent. It is symbolic that weddings can now take place in hotels, on football grounds and no doubt, before long, on racecourses. Perhaps someone could get a special booking to have their marriage in the studio while the lottery is being drawn ... or even better, during *Blind Date*. These are only symptoms of an unspiritual base to life. Even the word 'spiritual' is nearly lost, and can seem like a foreign language. Yet often there is much which is spiritual in the lives of the people who ask what it means. Life without the spirit is impoverished, and more people, young and older, are searching for that spirit today.

There are plenty of people who will latch onto this vacuum of spirit and offer to fill it with certainty. I seriously considered calling the book *Not the Nine O'Clock Service* as I listened to young people in Sheffield who had been deceived by their longing for certainty and absolute authority. There was much to appreciate in the worship and the community in the Nine O'Clock Service, but religion which depends totally upon the authority of an individual who offers certainty is always vulnerable to abuse. I want to encourage people not to delegate their own responsibility for deciding what is right and true, but work things out for themselves.

The danger in just thinking it out for ourselves is not recognizing any authority other than our own, and finding it difficult to belong to any wider community which expresses the same faith. In this way our world view and beliefs can become totally subjective and individualistic. It is also one of the problems of the age that there is a common disregard for authority of any kind, which can mean that we only accept what agrees with our own point of view. As soon as we belong to a group or a community with beliefs, we have to surrender a little of our individuality, and recognize the authority that such a group needs to command. I doubt, if we were to search for the whole of our days for a club, community, movement or group, which totally expresses what we ourselves believe to be true, we would ever find it. There has to be a proper humility about believing, but that humility should not provide an excuse to abdicate our own personal duty to think, or test out the corporate creeds to which we subscribe, and the way they are applied.

I have written this book between the fiftieth anniversaries of VE Day and VJ Day. The cause of that war was the people giving absolute authority to a Führer, or to a divine emperor. All those arms raised in 'Sieg Heil' in Germany, and the worship of the Rising Sun in Japan, expressed some desire for infallible authority, which is a denial of our God-given freedom and responsibility. It is only too easy to see such movements in other nations, without noticing what is corrupting or degrading our own. Jesus said, 'Where your treasure is, there will your heart be also.' How would our present society stand up to that rigorous test? Once the conditions were right, it only took a few years for Hitler to come to power. The people saw him as their saviour and it was a heady mixture even for a civilized and industrious nation. But it could happen to anyone. We can all be swept along by tides of thought and feeling. It is urgent that we think for ourselves and together find some sort of coherent vision for the future.

I was charmed by some research done in Islington.

Question:
'Do you believe in God?'
Answer:
'Yes.'
Question:
'Do you believe in a God who can intervene in people's lives and change them?'
The overwhelming reply was

'No, just the ordinary one!'

A set of powerful secular ideas dominate our society. Rather than seeing the universe as a 'creation' by God, the whole system is commonly seen in what we call scientific terms. By contrast, our religious language doesn't seem to be convincing. Religion is often portrayed as something to bring comfort to the weak, the neurotic, and the suffering, so it can appear not to be needed by the healthy and strong for whom the scientific descriptions appear to be enough to go on with. To many people it seems clear that eventually science will describe all that needs to be described. As this vast shift to the secular mind has happened, some theologians have tried to ride with it and lead people to God 'beyond God', writing books with titles like *The Death of God*, *The Secular Gospel* and in more recent years the work of Don Cupitt in *Sea of Faith*.

This process has being going strong for many generations and even more strongly in the 30 years I have been a priest and bishop. Belief in God was marginalized and the secular attitude established, which has left God as a back number for so many people. If the younger generation have missed out on God so far, it's largely the fault of my generation.

The secular denial of God can itself be raw prejudice. It is not only the Christian faith and belief in God which have to stand up to reality and criticism, but also the alternatives of agnosticism and atheism. I shall deal in very few certainties but, I hope, provide some probabilities and some assurance that the path of truth and faith is exciting and essential to the full life of personal freedom and commitment. We see already that people are beginning to look for something richer in spirit than the secular view. In this book, I shall remember that the young did not invent the secular mind, but rather received it as their inheritance.

In 1966 I had prepared, with nervous but excited anticipation, my first Good Friday meditation, to be given in our East London church. Sixteen people came, whilst 30,000 walked by the door to watch West Ham play at Upton Park. The post-war period has seen a great decline in church-going, though the people who now go to worship are often much more personally committed. (And as a consequence it's much more fun!) Although many of the surveys show that a large majority in our society still believe in God and want their children to be given religious instruction, God is, for the non-church-going majority, a pale shadow of his former self, perhaps a momentary guest at a wedding, or a moment of comfort at a funeral. People constantly reiterate clichés or repeat the old familiar questions, without taking the trouble to seek out the answers: 'You don't have to go to church to be a Christian'; 'There are so many religions, they can't all be true'; 'Church-goers are such hypocrites.' As a young woman said to me in a televised debate on Easter Day, 'There is no place in my life for God. What relevance can something that happened two thousand years ago possibly have for me *now*? If God is a God of love, why does he allow so much suffering in the world?'

Sometimes these are just excuses for putting the discovery of God on the back burner.

I shall question secular prejudice and encourage the sleeping religious imagination to consider the dimension of God. I do so with some optimism because I detect a real thirst for the spirit. For many it will require a major change in the way they think about the whole of their lives, whereas for others the locked gate to God will quietly slip open. Religion was once described as the opium of the people, but the materialist appetite is a powerful and damaging opiate to which people without a sense of spiritual identity and purpose are especially susceptible. Its propaganda has never been so persistent and all-pervasive.

I am hopeful against all the odds because I often meet young people who are already building up resistance to propaganda and developing spiritual antibodies to combat it. I meet them in church, on trains, in universities, in radio and TV studios and pubs. I hope this book may stir them up and invigorate their souls.

It is also important that anyone exploring God puts their whole self into the process. I am not asking you to suspend your beliefs, but to be open to recognize that if there is a God, then he has already been at work, loving you in your life. Part of the excitement of faith is the way so much of what we once saw as despair, failure, or weakness, begins itself to be seen to have a real purpose in the full journey.

Climbing mountains is exciting, awe-inspiring, but it brings profound satisfaction and discovering God is much the same. There too we have to begin at the beginning.

Two

In the Beginning

What was there in the beginning? Was there a beginning at all? As I type these ancient questions on the computer, I am just using a tool. I don't understand how the computer was made or how it works, and I am happy to use its capacity to write my book. But when I reflect upon it and what it can do, I am amazed. It seems little short of a miracle that it can store so much in its memory, can follow instructions, can do jobs in a few seconds which would previously have taken months. I realize that the computer has emerged through human intelligence working on the raw material of the universe. It required someone to discover the potential, and then design, make and programme it. Now it only requires a minute level of skill from me to do the job I want it to do. The fact of the matter is that I use many things in my life without asking how they work or how they are made, let alone why they should exist at all. The one thing I assume is that the computer is not some random part of an accidental process. Yet that's what many people assume about the universe – that it is some gigantic accidental process which just happened and from which everything follows.

Human beings have always tried to discover how things came to be, how they were made and how they work. Most of the things we use derive from shrewd copying and development of what already exists in the world and universe around us. As soon as we design or make something we look at it as though it was a 'creation', yet it emerges from what is already given. The human race has discovered the nature of much that exists and found ways of copying, manipulating, building from those ingredients.

For our survival, we have to learn how things work. We have to discover the effects that the things we make will have on everything else. But there is another key question ... not just *how* but *why* do they exist? What is their purpose? Will they be for the ultimate benefit of the universe? How will they change the meaning and overall well-being of our lives? So many times we have pursued the question 'how?', without asking the question 'why?'

Stephen Hawking finishes *A Brief History of Time* with these words:

> The people whose business it is to ask 'why', the philosophers, have not been able to keep up with the advance of scientific theories. In the eighteenth century, philosophers considered the whole of human knowledge, including science, to be their field and discussed questions such as: did the universe have a beginning? However, in the nineteenth and twentieth centuries, science became too technical and mathematical for the philosophers, or anyone else except a few specialists.

It's essential, however, that we should not panic but should go on asking 'why?' We should not be afraid of the specialists. We all need to be our own philosophers and theologians. Just because great academic works are written about theology doesn't mean we give up on exploring God. In the same way the advances of science do not disqualify us from asking the 'why?' questions. It's our life here and now which we have to direct and test.

We have the skill to split the atom, but that does not solve the problem as to whether we should. We can keep a human body ticking over in a persistent vegetative state, but that does not solve the problem of when to switch off the machine. Our capacity to design and build technology immediately leads to a moral dimension, where we have to ask serious questions about the consequences of our actions, and the reasons for doing them within the context of the meaning of our lives. These questions apply to the beginning of the universe. There is not only 'how?' did it happen, but also 'why?' and 'Why God?'

The questions about a first cause of the universe, its design and purpose, have an ancient history which does not come within the scope of this book. But the question and arguments go on reappearing. It is difficult for us to conceive of something just existing without a first cause. There is a deep-rooted need to believe there is a sufficient cause for everything. That's what we constantly perceive and it's the way our rational minds most often work. We believe we can trace things back to their origin and many find the whole idea of the universe either being infinite, or just happening, impossible or at least extremely difficult to accept. The question 'Why God?' has also been answered because of the belief that there must be an ultimate cause sufficient to account for what we now see. We are still up against the question. The search will go on to discover what there was before the Big Bang. How can we cross over to the reality from which the Big Bang, time and space emerged? The scientist may open the door, but it may lead into just another room with a door leading off that. So far, it can only be a matter of belief that there has to be a sufficient cause of everything that has happened – just as it must be a matter of belief that the universe emerged from nothing or from infinity.

The argument that the universe demonstrates the existence of a designer and a purpose also keeps reappearing. For example, William Paley's *Evidence of Christianity* at the end of the eighteenth century claimed that there must be a designer of the universe. He argued that the intricate construction of the eye suggests that there must be a master craftsman who created it. He concluded that if the universe showed the same signs of design and mechanical regularity as a watch then there must be a divine watchmaker. But this argument has been countered by showing how the apparent design can be explained by the evolutionary development driven by natural selection. Alongside this there is all the waste and signs of disorder and chaos to suggest a *blind* watchmaker. I do not believe either argument is proved. There is evidence pointing in both directions. Evolution may be the way in which God carries out his design. When looking at the way so much of human technology is achieved by understanding the way the universe works, it's not surprising that the argument from design to a designer is kept alive. Of course it raises problems for theology because it places responsibility for suffering and waste on the divine designer. This will not stop us sensing intuitively that the eye, the brain, the dragon-fly and the tortoise are *creatures* rather than random accidents.

The idea of 'purpose' in the universe is not susceptible of scientific testing. Yet it is one of the most profound spiritual needs that there be a purpose to existence. Most of us operate as though there is purpose in the lives we lead. A lack of purpose denies or at least erodes our values and reduces life to mere existence. It can be argued that the idea of purpose in the universe is a projection of our own longing and hope but, as we've seen before, the fact that something coincides with our need does not mean it is not real. We're best advised to look to drama, poetry, music and theology for purpose rather than to science.

But before we go any further, let's think for a moment what sort of evidence we would require to believe something to be true. People often say 'prove it', as though anything that can't be proved should not be believed. It's why I think St Thomas is a good candidate to be the patron saint of our generation. When told by his friends that Jesus had risen from the dead, he exclaimed: 'Unless I see the mark of the nails on his hands, unless I put my finger into the place where the nails were and my hand into his side, I will not believe it' (John 20.25).

We can perhaps sympathize with Thomas. It is, however, a cliché to suggest that we should only believe what we can prove in some scientific way. The technology of virtual reality is a useful reminder that everything is not always what it seems. There are those aspects of reality we cannot prove, but which we have to rely on daily, and we must accept that many things we see are not what they appear. A chair may be described as a solid object, but we know that in another view of its reality it is a mass of inner movement. For several millennia people only thought that star spoke to star because of their belief in the creation and the reality of God, but now we can observe galaxies as boiling cauldrons of activity which pour out matter and radiation of all wavelengths at unimaginable rates. We are fortunate in living in a quiet backwater in a remote area of our galaxy. We can also turn a switch on a TV and hear sounds and see pictures which are transmitted on waves, and we take it for granted because we are so used to the idea. But these facts are no more real now, because we know them, than they were when people just believed them out of faith. Scientific propositions cannot be proved. Everything hinges on experimental evidence which is never final. It only describes what has hitherto been the case.

But it is not only in the physical world that we have to base our lives on things we cannot prove. Some of the most important foundations of our thinking and acting cannot be proved either. For example, take the simple expression 'I did it because I thought it was right.' When we come to look at justice, morality and values we are not dealing with ideas that can be proved. They are matters of belief. We can't even claim that it is right because of our experience. In the end we have to take a massive step in the dark on the fragile basis of what we believe to be true. Dietrich Bonhoeffer, a German pastor convicted of plotting to kill Hitler, walked to his execution in 1945 with the words, 'This is not the beginning of the end, but the end of the beginning.' He made a martyr's death on the basis of his faith. He had no proof that there was life after death and nor do we, but his experience and his belief gave him the trust that what he believed was true. Sometimes we believe we ought to act in a particular way, in spite of the evidence that the result may not be good, but because we believe it is our responsibility to do so. We cannot prove that we ought to try and tackle poverty and hunger and other forms of injustice in our world. Indeed if we viewed the issue from the immediate perspective of our own material well-being we might decide just to get on with our own short lives and enjoy it while we may, but we are driven by what we believe is right and will be right in the long run; not just for ourselves, but for our world and our children's world as well as for the hungry and the homeless.

Our beliefs about what is right are not capable of proof, and yet we have to base so much of our lives upon them.

The same point can be made in our thinking about history. There is an old chestnut of a history exam question: 'The ninth century has been called the Dark Ages ... A lot can happen in the dark. Discuss!'

I have learnt from living with a professional historian just how difficult it is to prove facts about the past. There may be no evidence, or almost none, to work on. It can be like a train going into a tunnel and coming out the other side. The historian has to gather what evidence is available to make a shrewd assessment of what might have happened in the tunnel. Or there may be lots of evidence, but part of the evidence may cast serious doubt upon whether the people providing it were telling the truth because of their own bias. Or the witnesses may be genuinely confused and, because they didn't understand what was happening, describe what they saw in a way which looks to later generations to be deliberately misleading.

We had an example of these difficulties at our home in Stepney. A serious heist was taking place though the wall of our garage when we came home from holiday. Several men were involved. It was dangerous and exciting, and it all happened in a few moments. When the police arrived, they asked us as a family to describe what we had seen. How many men were there? Were they black or white? What clothes were they wearing? The pained look on the policeman's face, as these two adults and two children tried to agree any of these basic points, made us realize how confusing we found it trying to visualize what had happened to us. If someone had asked us two days later, we would have probably been even more confused. Yet the frightening event had happened. We could see the large hole in the garage wall and there were dangerous looking crow-bars left by the thieves, and there was a quarter of a million pounds worth of television sets missing from the warehouse next door. The one thing which we did remember was the number of the getaway lorry. This vulnerability of evidence is not just significant in such dramatic circumstances, but is around us every day.

So much of what is important in history goes on inside

people's minds or feelings. A historian may have an ancient seal which proves that Henry the Eighth gave a large property to one of his wives, but the reason why he gave it may be totally unknown. He may have had some cunning long-term motive in his mind, or it may have been that he woke up one morning and felt full of the joys of spring and just had to give her something. I also notice that the bits of hard evidence are often the most nondescript and insignificant things, whereas the things we really want to know about the past are buried with the people who lived through the events.

You may ask, 'Why bother with history, when it is so vulnerable?' The answer is that history is important for now and the future. In the 1980s I was chairing a group organizing the Auschwitz exhibition in East London. We hoped that it might tackle some of the racist and neo-Nazi views which infected those children growing up in an atmosphere of racial conflict. We had arguments amongst ourselves about the evidence and the way it should be presented. We had arguments with governments who did not want to subscribe to the suggestion that anti-Semitism had preceded Hitler. We still had survivors of the Holocaust to help us put the story together, but we also had propaganda on the streets that the Holocaust was a lie. History is vulnerable, but intensely important. We shall have to think about this when we move on from the more general discussion about the existence of God to the more specific questions about Jesus; because it is one of the distinctive aspects of the Christian faith that it depends upon historical events, and expects its adherents to base their lives and their actions upon those events. At this moment I am trying to show that this too is something which in the end, after thorough exploration, we have to trust rather than prove. We would be very hard-pressed if somehow we based our world view only on what we believed could be proved beyond all possible doubt to be true.

There is one more example of this (having to believe what is not proven) which is perhaps the most important of all. It concerns those three little words which St Paul called the three greatest virtues: faith, hope and love. Take these three experiences out of our lives and we'd be left with something inhuman. I can think of experiences of pleasure and material comfort which I have enjoyed, and often life just ticks over in a nondescript sort of way, but without any doubt the most important and precious experiences of my life have involved faith, hope and love. A friend or a parent will do many ordinary jobs for a child as an expression of faith, hope and love. The real trouble comes when your life is robbed of this meaning, so that you never have to do anything for anyone, or are never given opportunity to have convictions and ideas, or have to live without hope.

Yet faith, hope and love are based on aspects of life which cannot be proved. When two people get married, they make promises to each other. They may have lots of evidence that this is the person they want to spend their lives with. Or they may only feel enough trust to make a temporary commitment, precisely because they are so unsure of the other person or of themselves. They may be full of doubts about whether their love will last, or whether the person is trustworthy, or whether they are going to have enough money to manage. They may try the relationship out, but come to the conclusion that it won't work. Our relationships depend upon our believing and trusting in people though we still know so little about ourselves and each other. Two people may travel through the whole of their lives together and still not know all that there is to be known, and certainly not be able to prove that the commitment was going to work, without faith, hope and love. Faith is not the same as knowledge, though it is usually based on significant evidence. Hope, by definition, is a virtue which arises in the face of the possibility of its opposite. Love carries prodigious risks but without it life is nothing.

I have tried to show that we proceed through life having to trust in many unprovable judgements. This is so in the physical world, in history, in morality, in faith, hope and love. We often have to believe without proof on the basis of what is sometimes quite fragile or conflicting evidence. This is part of the vulnerability of our lives, and indeed is part of the adventure which makes life worthwhile and dangerous and fraught with struggle and joy.

Scientists need to have faith. They too need vision and insight into what is actually there. It was said of Faraday that 'he smells the truth'. The scientist too must trust that the universe is intelligible and consistent over space and time. In many ways faith and science are partners.

Now I can return to my theme and think about the creation and God. I find the exploration of the origins of our world and the universe awe-inspiring. During most of my adult life there has been a conflict between the Steady State and Big Bang theories. Nowadays the Big Bang theory is in the ascendancy and the physicists and mathematicians describe, in what sometimes seems like religious language, the way our universe came to be. Indeed why should it not be religious language if it explores the deepest origin of things? There are very few quotations in this book, but one that is essential comes from Einstein:

> The most beautiful and profound emotion we can experience is the sensation of the mystical. It is the dower of all true science. He to whom this emotion is a stranger, who can no longer wonder and stand wrapped in awe, is as good as dead. To know that what is impenetrable to us really exists, manifesting itself as the highest wisdom and the most radiant beauty, which our dull faculties can comprehend only in the most primitive forms, this knowledge, this feeling is the centre of true religion.

To explore the truth about the way things are leads us often to feelings of awe and wonder, which are at the root of so much religious experience throughout human history. When asked what came before the Big Bang, a young lecturer researcher, who spoke with something akin to visionary fervour, said that as far as one could see, which was not far, the Big Bang was preceded by radiant light. There is still so much to explore. No one knows what we shall find. I had the chance to ask the same question on Internet. This is the answer given in October 1995:

> The answer is simply: 'We don't know.' As one goes back in time, the material in the universe becomes denser and denser as well as hotter and hotter.

Eventually, one reaches the point at which things are so dense and so hot that our current understanding of the laws of physics are unable to make predictions about what occurs.

In order to know what happened 'before the Big Bang' or even to know if that question makes sense, requires advances in our understanding of high-energy physics and will remain open until this understanding is reached. (Joseph Wang)

I am not trying to show that in some way the new scientific account fits with the Bible's account, because the Bible is not a scientific book. It is a book about the meaning of things, and tackles the reason *why* things came to be, and only secondarily does it say *how*. It uses the poetry, legends and understanding of ancient people. It may be that in the beginning the Earth was a vast waste and darkness, and that then there was radiant light, and it may be there is a wonderful resonance with the Bible account of creation; but the central point that the writers are making is that God made it, that it is a creation not an accident. It is a purposeful, creative act of almighty power and, when God created it, he saw that it was good. I am trying to help us face the ultimate question as to whether the whole of existence is an extraordinary accident or an extraordinary purposeful act of creation. Whether we talk about the vast scale of the universe or the micro-scale of DNA, the question persists. I came across this description of DNA as 'an impersonal, unreflective, robotic, mindless little scrap of molecular machinery. It is the ultimate basis of all the agency, and hence meaning, and hence consciousness, in the universe.'

On the other hand there is a sense of wonder when you read that this 'mindless little scrap of molecular machinery' in the human body is over a metre long. It contains 3.3 billion base pairs and, if it was magnified to a hundredth of an inch thickness, it would be 75 miles long. On the one hand we are faced by 'impersonal, unreflective, robotic' material, yet on the other by something so stunning in micro-engineering that it leads us to feelings of awe.

It is not surprising therefore that many young people have

said to me that they cannot 'imagine' a creator. This derives from our success in scientific explanations, together with the collapse of the religious imagination. The old pictures of God seated on a throne, high and lifted up in heaven, whether painted by artists, poets or sculptors, or from accounts given in the Bible, have failed to convince many people in a materialist and secular age. This is so serious that some theologians have thought we had to give it up altogether. 'Our image of God must go' was the headline which shocked us in the sixties. Some claimed that God or the idea of God was dead, and they hoped that we could grow out of this archaic way of looking at God. They said we needed a much more secular view. They believed that God was primarily to be discovered inside ourselves or in loving our neighbour, or in the 'ground of being'. But this raises for us the question as to whether there is a dimension of God which is real and is distinct from the dimensions of the universe which can be measured or observed and recorded. Is there another sort of reality beyond time and space?

I am not claiming to prove without doubt that there is a hidden dimension of God, but rather to show that it is reasonable to believe that there is what has been called 'eternal' life. Whether we are atheists, agnostics, or religious believers, we all have to change our understanding of the way things are, as we further our knowledge. It's not surprising that sometimes we are afraid to change because it looks so disturbing. It's not difficult to see why people who had always believed that the Earth was flat and at the centre of the universe, were threatened by the idea that it was a spinning sphere and just a small part of the solar system. Though the idea that the universe originated with a Big Bang is equally disturbing, secular people are now less shaken by it than they would have been 100 years ago. I think it is encouraging that the younger generation are more open to receiving new understanding of the way things are. In tackling these ultimate questions, prejudice against religious insights is as foolish as prejudice against scientific perception. The religious insight attempts to describe in pictures, parables and myths this other dimension. My question is how this dimension can become real again for us now, in a fresh way.

As I understand it, there is vivid change taking place in the way we perceive time and space. To put it in the simplest terms, it has been a common idea that somehow space and time had always existed. It was thought there had been infinite time in infinite space. According to the Big Bang theory, we are to believe that space and time expanded within the process of the Big Bang itself, and are still expanding. If what we now see, and can measure, derives from an original compressed reality, then it is not inevitable that time and space are infinite. Indeed, science talks of the non-existence of time and space in the 'naked singularity' from which the known universe apparently evolved after the Big Bang. There was therefore a beginning of what we now experience. We don't know, however, what preceded that beginning. According to the present pictures scientists are using of reality, they can tell the timetable of the Big Bang down to 10^{-43} seconds, but a veil is still drawn across what happened or what existed before that. But 'before' is a quite meaningless word in this context and, to think about it, we need to suggest some other sort of dimension or even meta-time.

It is in itself almost unbelievable that the universe could have potentially existed in the compressed reality which exploded in the Big Bang. To my mind, it is rational to believe that this was an act of creation from the dimension of God. The old arguments for the existence of God claimed that there had to be a first cause, and that that cause had to be greater than, or at least capable of causing, what happened and existed. It is a strange irony that after all our knowledge, our searching and exploration, we are faced with much the same philosophical question as the primitive naked ape when he first began to think in an independent self-conscious way: 'Does God exist?'

The 'weak anthropic principle' notes that the laws of physics describe forces, masses and other quantities with numerical values which have been measured accurately. If any of the found values were different – in some cases by an exceedingly small fraction – life as we know it could not exist. In the universe our existence is exceedingly improbable. But it is the reality we see.

A child could ask (and often does), 'Who made God?' It's

a good question. By suggesting that there had to be God who caused it all, are we cheating? Are we just putting the problem of existence one further stage back? The child might say that one ancient answer was more honest: that God rested on an elephant, which rested on an elephant, which rested on a tortoise . . . and so on. But I don't believe that God is proposed as the cause of the universe simply in order to explain how it happened. The old arguments did not manage to prove the existence of God. In the end it depends upon faith not on proof. They demonstrated, however, that it was not unreasonable to believe in a creator if that creator required no cause but was Itself the cause of everything. Consider how difficult it will be for the atheist to explain how an accidental compressed reality, in a great demonstration of power, 'created' a universe – a universe capable of producing the mind that invented the computer. People often say to believers in God, 'Explain this', without seeing that they too should have their explanation ready; and not just *how* reality happened by *why* and what its purpose is.

Though randomness is fundamental to the universe and its physical and biological evolution, paradoxically chance brings about the order we see. There is poetic truth in the Genesis account of order emerging from chaos. The Earth emerged as a habitable planet out of the chaotic events of the Big Bang itself. There is also evidence of what were vast random events such as asteroid impacts or volcanic eruptions which caused mass extinctions and gave rise to another surge in evolution. Dinosaurs did not survive – other creatures did. It seems to have been a matter of having been in the wrong or right place at the right time. If we believe in God we have to take account of the substantial role of chance and accident in the life we receive from God, and if we do not believe in God we have to give some account of the emergence of rational beings and purpose.

This perplexing reality applies to the quite ordinary events of our daily life. We are trying day by day to impose order on chaos. It is a battle and there are moment-to-moment setbacks, but there is evidence that we are often successful (often overcoming the accidents and chances that happen), though sometimes not. It is at least as difficult to sustain the argument that the whole of creation is an accident as it is to sustain the belief that there is God, yet so many people seem to have been persuaded that this is not so. A developing faith, however, becomes more and more assured that through and beyond the 'changes and chances of this fleeting world' there is divine love; but that is to leap ahead.

When we use the old biblical pictures as though they were literal descriptions of God rather than a way of communicating the existence of a creator, many people reserve judgement. The evolution of the universe from a uniform soup of matter and energy through subatomic particles, simple atoms, galaxies, stars, complex atoms, molecules, planets with complex geology and inorganic chemistry, organic chemicals, self-replicating chemicals (and so life), cells, multicellular organisms and finally consciousness, does not sit easily with the personal human descriptions of God. We have to remember that the images we use of God on a throne are there to stir our imagination to conceive of the wonder and majesty of the God who it is believed created all this. Jesus asked the question: 'I have spoken to you of earthly things and you do not believe; how then will you believe if I speak of heavenly things?' (John 3.12). The personal analogy of God as father is essential to our souls, but it is not a laboratory sort of truth.

At both the macro- and micro-levels it is amazing how our knowledge has developed in this century. In space our vision extends from the sub-components of atomic particles to a universe of thousands of millions of galaxies. We can look back and see the early universe and the Big Bang. We can describe, too, the intricate molecular mechanism of living cells. It is an extraordinary privilege to have such knowledge, incomplete though it is. As the mystery unfolds, at every point, the scale and richness of the creation surpass anything man could have imagined. Yet with all this exciting and mind-blowing knowledge the suggestion is still that each new property appears to have emerged as a consequence of the properties of the previous stage – that the 'singular' beginning contained the potential for all the subsequent development. To think and pray about these things is awe-inspiring and in my experience leads to worship of the God whom we call father.

If it is not irrational to believe in a first cause, which was and is sufficient to account for the reality we see, then it is a proper question to ask in what sort of reality does this first cause and sustainer of the universe exist? Perhaps eventually the scientists will discover that the compressed reality containing the potential for time and space had to emerge from a different way of being, which may give us clues to the eternal dimension of God. Meanwhile we have another vast range of evidence that this other reality exists in the religious experience of human kind.

Is it possible that there is another dimension, a sort of reality, not tied as we are in this life to time and space? This other invisible dimension of God, sometimes called God's Kingdom, sometimes eternity, is often dismissed by present generations because of a prejudice derived from secular attitudes and from mistaken ideas of what can be known, or cannot be known, of what can be proved and what cannot be proved and therefore what can be believed. We do not know what is the source of everything. But the personal direct question is: can we get in touch with it? We claim as believers that it is possible for us to taste eternal life, to relate to God the creator and sustainer of the universe. So I now want to call on the evidence of the human experience which is called 'religious'.

From the first appearance of human beings on earth there has been a sense of an invisible dimension. This sense of the holy has stirred ideas and images of divine beings in paradise. Not only have humans believed in this unseen dimension of gods, but they have sensed that their lives and the existence of the rest of perceived reality somehow depended upon it. They have seen their world as intimately related to it. It is not until relatively recently in human history that people have claimed that this invisible dimension did not exist, that it was an invention, or illusion invented by human beings to explain the inexplicable. It is a relatively new idea that God was invented to ease their psychological needs and fears, assuage their guilt, and offer immortality in the face of death. This 'illusion' is said to have been part of human growing up.

It is claimed that now we have 'come of age'. We can thus finally be free of this god of the gaps and face up to reality as it plainly is. We must make the best of existence through education and justice programmes. We must search for happiness in the life we are given, without 'pie in the sky when you die'.

This 'freedom' from God and the invisible dimension should apparently have had the result of making us care more about each other and the world we share. It was supposed to free us from the neurosis of some power outside ourselves which questions our independence and creates a secret file on our identity. This atheistic view appears quite often in the far less acceptable guise of pride, selfishness and amorality, but that is not my concern at this moment. As we have discovered in interfaith relationships, it is wrong to compare the best fruits produced in the garden of your own faith with the worst fruits produced in the garden of another faith. All faiths (including atheism) can be misused, distorted and become a playground for evil, but in this book I am trying to discover what is true and good and just. Therefore it is important to see the strength of the atheist position as well as its weakness. It is also important to see the weakness of the believer's position, otherwise we shall soon be disillusioned. It was Bishop David Jenkins who said that all Christians should be dis-illusioned and he was right, because our faith has to be built on reality. This does not mean that we should limit reality to our own knowledge and understanding, nor prohibit the use of our imagination and experience in our search for God, but that our search has to be carried out in an honest way, admitting our limitations.

What sort of evidence is religious experience? Perhaps it's wise first to recognize its vulnerability. The line between sick and healthy religion can be blurred. Although I had seen this grim fact in ordinary life, it came home to me with frightening clarity when working in a mental hospital with mentally sick people. The illness often took the form of religious mania. Perhaps this is one reason why some clinical psychiatrists have found religion dangerous, and why faith is rarely offered by that profession as a source of strength to the chronically anxious and despairing. Others, of course, have found the search of the subconscious mind a window into the dimension of God. Religious experience does have great power, and is therefore capable of great distortion. But even distorted vision can contain truths that are important to us. Even if the gate of heaven is unhinged, it may be possible to catch a glimpse through it. People who have the greatest struggle with their lives often show us depths which more mundane lives do not notice. Sick religion, however, happens. But then love itself can become obsessive or dangerous in a sick mind, though that is no reason to give up on love. We don't give up on sex because bad sex exists, we look for wholesome sex within loving relationships. We need to be on our guard against the perversion of religion, but not fear true religion as a result. Religious experience is a very subjective thing and, as Jeremiah warned us, 'the heart is deceitful above all things'.

Jeremiah might also have said that the heart is honest above all things. We don't say about a great poet that he had vivid experience of good and evil and therefore what he writes has no truth in it. We know within ourselves that with all our struggles and mistakes and blindness, we also have the capacity to glimpse truth, to experience a love greater than we had imagined and to perceive beauty in a way that inspires us. Life remains precious because we have the capacity to see and appreciate and respond to truth, beauty and goodness. Although we can be deceived and defeated by the evil imagination within us, we nevertheless trust that we can search for the truth. We may do everything we can to explore the experience of others, and the observable world, but we remain convinced that our own views have value, even though at root they are inevitably subjective ... that is, they arise in the confusion and feelings and needs of our own personality. When we love someone, we act according to our highest self, and yet that love is a mixture of a wide range of thoughts, feelings, needs and personal experiences. We do not say that our love is untrue because it stems from a vulnerable human personality. So subjectivity may be a reason for caution about the nature of religious experience as evidence for the existence of the dimension of God, but it is no reason for writing off the evidence entirely.

Another problem with using the evidence of religious experience for the existence of God's dimension is the fact that religious experience is so diverse, and often appears to be contradictory. It has always seemed upside-down to me to say, 'There are so many different religions, God can't be true.' There are so many different expressions of almost every important issue in our lives that it would seem absurd to say that we can't believe something because it has taken so many different forms. That's just what I would expect it to do. Look just for a moment at another essential area of our lives ... politics! Politicians make a virtue out of showing how different their manifestos are. There's no greater insult than to suggest that one party agrees with another.

Cultures have all developed in wondrously varied ways and produced different windows onto God. As I know from practical experience, many of these religions have far more in common than some people are willing to admit. There is a lot of similarity in moral teaching and there are very similar experiences in prayer and meditation. They all try to produce ways of creating goodness and defeating evil, and they all call their followers to holiness of life. Apart from Buddhism, all the major religions have one massive idea in common: namely, that there is God and God's dimension. This great idea is subject to all sorts of interpretation. People care passionately about the truth seen through their own culture, so there is often conflict, but so it is with all our cross-cultural experience. But if we manage to cross the boundaries between faiths, we find an exciting strength. It is certainly the hope of Christianity that we shall find, in God's dimension, unity in diversity: neither race, nor creed, nor class, nor nation will divide us. Religion can be used by people for any purpose of power or greed or nationalism, but then so can all the other ideas and energies of the human race. This does not of itself make religious experience untrue.

The experience of the dimension of God has taken myriad forms. It can range from ecstasy – a being exalted out of oneself – to a quiet accumulation of assurance about the existence of God through a life of prayer. It can consist of a traumatic conversion of a passionate and dramatic kind or be like the steady flow of a river through a meadow. It can be a secret learnt in giving birth to a child or a deep understanding given in the death of a loved one. It can be found in intellectual turmoil or in simple wonder. It is about the growing conviction that there is God and that God is in another dimension which is intimately related to us. This experience gives meaning and purpose to our lives and demonstrates to us that we are not alone but are dependent on God for our being. It gives rise to feelings of great adoration and joy and a sense of beauty and hope, without leaving a hangover in the morning!

However much we argue about the existence of God and the eternal dimension, most of us do not come to faith by argument, but rather by relationship and encounter with the Spirit of God. The writer of the book of Job in the Old Testament sets out the traditional arguments. Job's comforters claim that these arguments explain why he suffers. He refutes their answers and maintains that his treatment by God is unjust, but in the end he encounters God and all his arguments fade away. 'I have spoken of things which I have not understood, things too wonderful for me to know ... I knew of you then only by report, but now I see you with my own eyes. Therefore I yield, repenting in dust and ashes' (Job 42.3–6). In the Christian era two thousand years later than Job, another giant of theology and one of the most influential thinkers of all time, St Thomas Aquinas, attempted to prove the existence of God on the basis of the teaching of Aristotle. When he finished his great work in prayer and love of God, he had an experience of God which far transcended the construct of his mind and said, 'All that I have written appears to be as so much straw after the things that have been revealed to me.' The Bible is a book of encounters with God. As such, it not only encourages us in our exploration of God, but is also a way to check out what we experience, not like a highway code or book of instructions, but an inspiration to stir up and test the love that is already being born within us.

Before I believed, it used to strike me as unfair that religious people in argument often resorted to personal experience – experience which I had not had. In a way that is bound to be, because God, if there is God, is bound to be greater than our thoughts and arguments about Him. It is unlikely that the creator of the universe is going to be neatly summed up by a human being, however intelligent or wise that human being may be. To debate and take trouble to think about God is rather like walking up the foothills of a mountain. I've found this a helpful parable in dialogue with people of other faiths. The higher part of the mountain is shrouded in mist, but it has a fascination and we are drawn on, and sometimes we are surprised by the mist clearing and we are given a breathtaking view of the way to the peak. It soon mists over again, but now we are hooked.

Another great philosopher, Blaise Pascal, said that someone who searches for God has already found him. Although all the arguments were for me transcended by the encounter with God, I care passionately that we are engaged in a search for truth. If we deny the truth we see, we shall not come to the source of truth, whom we do not see. I used to think that part of belief in God was the willingness to accept that tomorrow I may be convinced that God is not true; but I have to be honest with you and say that I do not think now that I shall ever become an unbeliever again. As long as we are honest, we can travel along together because there is so much we both don't know. Perhaps it's more like a journey to a great, largely unknown continent which far transcends our own experience: we explore it together, bringing our own ideas and experience with us, but both stunned by what we see and learn on the trip. Whether or not you are willing to come along is your choice but I hope you will make the trip with someone. God is a continent infinitely worth finding.

Three

What sort of God?

There are millions of searchers for God. They come up with all sorts of answers. Mormons, Jehovah's Witnesses, New Age Travellers, Druids, neo-Pagans, the cults and the seekers and adherents of the mainline religions, each have their own answers. The answers they find regarding the nature and character of the divine vary enormously and have a variety of effects on followers. What we worship in life has considerable power over the people we become. So 'What sort of God?' is a key question.

I hope we can begin the next stage of the exploration at least by agreeing that it is not unreasonable to believe in God and in the invisible dimension of God. I have tried to show that it is unlikely that we shall be able to prove God's existence but, in our search for the truth together, we are going to have to opt for what seems 'probable' to us. The belief in God proposes that the universe is a creation, not an accident. This obviously has enormous implications for the way we look at our lives. I have also accepted that reasoned argument can only take us so far. In the end, faith is not about proofs and debates but about encounter with God.

Belief is not an abstract idea which you can happily take or leave. The existence of God is bound to affect our perception of everything we are, we say, and do. It reaches right into the heart of being itself. As the Bible says, it reaches to 'where joint and marrow divide' (Hebrews 4.12). It is important therefore to have a clear idea as to what sort of God we are talking about. We have to be able to defend our idea of God in the face of the reality we all see. If we were Satanists, we would have to give some account of the universal longing for the good. If we believed in a functional, amoral God we would have to give some account of the fact that we are moral beings. We would also have to think about whether there is one God or many; whether God is a divided cabinet, or a dictatorship. The nature of God has profound influence upon those who claim to be disciples. God has to be tested against experience and, if we have faith, reality has to be tested against God. This too is a process that has gone on from the beginning.

This would be a very long book if it included a history of the idea of God. Perhaps I could just give three examples.

The most obvious is the idea that nature itself is God. This has taken many forms and draws its strength from human experience of the awesome wonder of nature itself. It is not difficult when faced with a mountain or the sea, or an eagle or a bull, or when caught in a storm or in a dark wood, to think of God. We also have this sense of awe when our own human control of our environment runs out: in an earth-quake or a hurricane, or on a boat hurled about by the ocean, let alone the power expressed in the Big Bang. It seems such a pity that they changed the African name 'The Mighty Thunderer' to 'Victoria Falls'.

The idea that God is nature and nature is God has many weaknesses, although it is still popular. If nature is God, many questions have to be answered. The laws of nature of themselves do not offer any moral vision. In the end the existence of such a god will be determined by extreme heat or cold of the Earth and the god will die. How do believers in a nature god cope with a god whose character appears sometimes to be cruel, wasteful and is constantly recycled? How is it that the human mind, although making catastrophic mistakes in the stewardship of nature, at the same time has developed such mastery over many of its powers? How far is this god identified with nature itself or does it represent some spirit who lies behind nature? If it does, what is the character of that spirit? As we shall see, other religions have to cope with some of these problems as well, but not in such extreme form.

It is not surprising that the three great world religions which have their roots in Abraham — that is, Judaism,

Christianity and Islam — have all been opposed to the worship of nature itself. God judged the people of Israel in the wilderness because they rejected the invisible God in favour of the golden calf which symbolized material prosperity, fertility and nature's power. Their great mistake was to worship the creation rather than the invisible creator, to worship the stars rather than the one who set them on their courses, to worship gold rather than the one who gave such gifts, to put the instincts in the place of the moral vision of the invisible God. These idols still survive: for instance, in the 'outstretched arm' of the lottery, in the divinity attributed to market forces, and in the worship of sexuality. There is not so much difference between the primitive worship of nature, and our worship of the motor car and the seductive activities of our advertisers. I think our modern worship of objects is far more universally damaging.

Another idea of God was that there were many gods. Different cultures developed different dynasties or families of gods. Homer, for instance, gave story and shape to the Greek gods of the classical period. If different gods are responsible for different aspects of life, such as war, hunting, feasting, love, elemental forces and the rest, it was also necessary to show how they interrelated or else chaos would follow. Homer gave the legendary framework which described the spheres of influence of each god and their relative power. Although Zeus was the greatest of the gods, his wishes could be seriously thwarted by the determination of a lesser god. When a ship set out on a journey, Zeus might regard the journey with favour but Poseidon, the god of the sea, might have been offended by the sailors, or indeed by Zeus himself, and the ship might be wrecked by the power of the high seas.

It is only too easy for our generations to mock these ancient ideas of God. However, if we see the work of the sculptors and architects of that culture, if we attend a play by Sophocles, or get absorbed in the *Odyssey* or realize how often philosophers return to Plato and Aristotle, then we have to think again. These gods may have collapsed in ruins but the harvest of their time demonstrates they emerged in a fertile period of the human spirit. The Greeks' pursuit of truth and beauty, their vivid imagination of the invisible dimension, their vision of civilization and the birth of democracy (even if just for an élite), the laying of foundations of philosophy, their celebration of the human, all point to the splendour of the classical period and therefore call for respect and understanding of the religion which fed and, for a while, sustained and inspired it. It recognized and gave expression to the conflicts and chaos in human experience, by projecting onto the gods all the basic beauty, emotions and rivalries of the human race. In a way it was a celebration of godhead in human form, or perhaps more accurately the celebration of the human in the kingdom of the gods.

There is a wonderful statue of Hermes in the museum at Olympia. He is standing holding a child. To us he appears to be a perfect specimen of a human male, but to his generation there were small, intimate signs, like his stance and his sandals, that he was a god. Here was a strength and a weakness. The strength was to give human expression to godhead, so that human beings were offered encouragement in their own ideals and hopes. The weakness followed from this in that the gods became snared and stained by bearing the flaws and sinfulness of the human experience. The gods went through the same chaos and drama and tragedy as we do, and ultimately became unbelievable as God. This period of flowering of the human spirit at a particular time in a particular place became one of the profound influences on the development of Christianity.

Another idea of God, which has had a long run, is the explanation of the existence of evil by the belief that there are two gods: one good and the other evil. Sometimes it was clearly one god, but on the Earth two spirits. Again this draws its strength from the fact that it seems to reflect the reality of our lives. It deifies the struggle between the forces of good and evil. Because there is so much suffering and wickedness in our world, it was not a long step to believing that the divinity of good was to be found in the eternal dimension. Humankind was thought to possess a spark of the divine light in the soul, which could only struggle to free itself from the stain of the lower nature. The Amnesty International symbol of a candle burning in coiled barbed wire provides a metaphor for the imprisoned state of the soul in its earthly toil. There followed, from this belief, ascetic practices for disciples as they prepared their souls for eternal life. This faith could include a negative view of creation, because nature itself was the snare for the soul. These ideas too fed into the stream of Christian development. It is a vivid example of how much what we believe about the nature of God affects the way we behave in this world. Dualism, as it is called, also had the strength drawn from recognizing the reality and extent of evil, which remains one of the main problems for the belief in one God. It is to this idea which I now turn.

It is important to give some setting to the main idea of God which concerns us in this book, and that is the idea that God is one. Monotheism has made great progress within the major faiths of the world, including those faiths such as Hinduism and Jainism where, at first sight, that does not seem to be the case. Although belief in one God alone has been so successful, it too has serious questions to answer. In the Bible, we can read about the historic battle for monotheism as it took literary shape in a very particular place and at roughly the same time as Homer was reflecting in his poetry the idea that there were many gods.

The journey from belief in many gods – gods of places, tribes, and myths; gods in nature, fertility, evil and other facets of human experience – to belief in there being only one God, creator of all, was a gigantic step for human kind. It was not made without great cost. It went through various stages, not in a neat orderly way but through the erratic steps of the human pilgrimage. It's important to remember that the story of this change is not told in historical sequence in the Bible. There are times when the God of Israel is spoken of as one amongst many gods, and times when he is spoken of as the greatest god of all; and then the idea grows that the God of Israel is the only God and the other gods do not exist – they are nothing. On the surface it seems such an absurd claim that the God of a twelve-tribe group in a small and insignificant region should be the universal God, but that's the way it was. Abraham came from the land of his fathers and received the promise as the friend of God that his descendants would be as numerous as the grains of sand on the seashore ... the covenant made with Abraham would have universal significance.

On Mount Horeb, God promised that he would bring the people of Israel out of slavery in Egypt to freedom. In one of those mountain experiences when the mist cleared for a human mind, God revealed his name to Moses. 'I am what I am. Tell the people of Israel that "I Am" has sent you' (Exodus 3.14). The name Yahweh or Jehovah is Hebrew for 'I Am' or 'I will be there'. By knowing the name of a person, you have the clue not only to their identity, but also to their character. God was revealed as the source of all being, and at the same time as a God who would 'be there' for the people of Israel. Later, on Mount Sinai, God revealed to Moses the way God expected the people to live in the Ten Commandments. After 40 years of wandering in the wilderness the people of Israel were settled in the land flowing with milk and honey. It was almost as though the idea of one God alone had made space for itself on Earth.

This process itself was fraught with dangers, hesitations and struggle, and it went on being so through several centuries of conflict and mistakes and rethinking. Then in the voice of the prophets the message rang out loud and clear (ironically at the time the Kingdom of Israel split and eventually was overwhelmed and its people sent again into exile). The full-scale idea that the God of Israel was a universal God blossomed.

Isaiah's vision in the temple demonstrated the worship of the great high God: 'Holy, Holy, Holy is the Lord of Hosts: Heaven and Earth are full of his glory' (Isaiah 6.3). Then, in the time of the exile, came the assertion of the truth of the Lord the creator. ' "To whom, then, will you liken me, whom set up as equal?" asks the Holy One. "Lift up your eyes to the heavens; consider who created these, led out their host one by one?" ' Over and over again he asserted that there is only one God and no other. He reinforces his argument by satirizing the idols. How could people really believe in a god made out of wood? When the carver of the idol finishes his work, he throws the rest of the wood on the fire – a god who could be burnt hardly seemed a possible creator of the universe. The old idea that there were many gods was absurd – there was only one, and that was the Lord. The battle went on against Baals, against local gods, against kings when they made themselves gods, and even against the people of Israel when they forgot or betrayed the trust they had been given. As we know, both Christianity and Islam took this faith in one God beyond its specifically Jewish focus, and it grew outside the confines of Israel.

This movement to the idea of God as one was also developing elsewhere in the world even where there were expressions of different aspects of God. I have, however, only given the briefest sketch of a long and complicated process to reflect on the idea of God being One and it's important now to look at whether this idea makes more sense of reality.

Although within the very substance of the material world there are strong negatives and positives which war against each other, or provide the tension from which much of the created order derives, the idea of different and independent divine sources of creation makes the idea of a universal operation almost unthinkable. Imagine a universe in which a god could set up different and contrary realities. It would be rather like the initial teething problem of rail privatization: a timetable which is uncoordinated, because one company says it's only responsible for one part of the region, without joining up with the rest, and another says it's going to run its trains in its own way, without careful cooperative planning. Although the universe demonstrates incredible diversity, science depends upon there being an underlying unity. We rely upon being able to explore on the basis of an inner coherence, in spite of all the myriad faces of reality. It is impossible to conceive of a Big Bang which enabled the existence of such a miraculous universe as this, and at this moment appears to have created a unique planet on which sentient life is conceived and sustained. It could not be the creation of conflicting driving powers. It's difficult to plan together a village fête, let alone a United Nations or a European State. If we try to imagine a committee of gods planning the universe, the idea breaks down into an absurdity.

But it is not just our pragmatic understanding which makes a divided god or alternative sources of power and purpose difficult, if not impossible, to believe; it is also because of our experience of prayer. Religious experience often brings an intense vision of unity in God. As always, we can't know how much of this intensity derives from the human desire for unity in the storms and conflicts of division and hatred in our world. Whether or not it stems from the reality of God himself, we have to account for the yearning itself. Not only do we have a longing to be united with another human being but many of us have a longing to be united in some mystical way with God. When Martin Buber, the Jewish philosopher, expressed this intimate relationship with the creator he chose to call it 'I ... Thou'. Prayer frequently takes the form of a longing for unity with God, for unity in God's world, and for unity with each other. It can also express the desire for unity in oneself.

The split personality presents us with one of the most painful challenges to an individual's well-being and personal relationships. When people go through this distress at first hand, they begin to see in a new and vivid way what a wonderful gift 'coherence' is. All of us experience some level of disunity in our thoughts and actions; we know what doubt and anxiety are like. We also get involved in conflicts we regret but we see it as a sign of health and well-being that, within this tension and stress, we maintain our own sense of being a united self. The experience of being torn in two is a source of emotional and mental pain. There is a wonderful passage in the story of Adam and Eve where the significance of unity between two people is described. God had created all the creatures of the Earth but Adam was alone. God removed Adam's rib and created, from the rib, a woman. Although this story offends some women, it's important not to lose the truth contained in it. Adam woke from sleep and said, 'This one at last is bone from my bones, flesh from my flesh!' He recognizes that here is a being with whom he can find the unity he desires. This story is not about sex, but even sex has within it a yearning for unity which produces dissatisfaction if it is not achieved.

It is fascinating too that so much of religious practice, in cult and worship and prayer, expresses the search for restoring unity with God. It even has a special theological name: 'atonement'. It is possible to suggest that this fear of separation is just an irrational feeling, and that in the longing for unity the human race is just fostering an illusion. If it is an illusion, however, it has had remarkable results in the lives of saints, martyrs and other believers through the ages. Over and over again we see the human battle for integrity as precious, and the more we see a person being able to hold together their identity in the face of division and conflict the more we respect them. Those of us who struggle with religious faith will bear witness that the process of returning to being at one with God is the key to our continued search for integrity, and it enables us to hold together our understanding of ourselves and the world around us. It expresses the profound reconciliation with being itself. Plural gods would at once and in a fundamental way undermine and fragment the coherence given by a single 'Thou' at the heart of our lives. As we shall see so often in this exploration, human need lies at the heart of belief. To some this demonstrates that it is an illusion; to believers it is more like our need for food, our need for love, our need for a meaning in life – they are signs of our design and origin in God. The human character he has given us searches for him. 'Our hearts are restless till they find their rest in Thee' (St Augustine).

A plurality of gods denies fundamental aspects of reality. It is as though there is some fundamental human conviction that, if there is God, God must be One. This unity of God, however, poses us with problems and these problems must now be examined.

The belief that God was One was accompanied by the developing idea that God was almighty and good. The power of God the creator was manifest to anyone who opened their eyes and ears. The God who set the planets and stars on their courses, who in his anger could rouse an earthquake, who was enthroned above the sky, who could bring the universe into being, must of necessity be, to all intents and purposes, all-powerful. But power, then as now, is a dangerous model to use because we see, as they saw, power being so prodigiously misused by those who possessed it and exercised it on earth. Ours is not the first generation to experience despair because human beings so often fail to use the power they are given in a wise, good and righteous way. Even that paragon of virtue and wisdom, Solomon, ended up as a man corrupted by power who misused it to oppress the people. So the hope grew that there would be a good, wise ruler, a wonderful counsellor, who would rule with justice, righteousness and care for the people. The prophets' role was to confront the kings and others with the judgement of God about the way they exercised their power. The judgement was based on their belief that God was almighty and all-good.

Alongside this conviction that God was almighty and all-good was the equally strong message that God was a God of mercy. One of his prime characteristics was that he exercised steadfast love. Alongside belief in the wrath of God roused by the sinfulness of man, grew the conviction that God would forgive the people who repented and changed their ways. This mercy and steadfast love was of the very essence of God. But the prophets were concerned to show that this mercy and love did not mean that God was soft on sin. His mercy did not in any way reduce his holiness. The problem was: how could God be forgiving and merciful if it meant not punishing people as they deserve? Wouldn't he himself become stained and seem to collude with the wickedness of humankind? Because God was so far above our understanding – the mysterious creator – he was surrounded by awe and ritual. Human beings could only approach with great caution, removing their shoes because this was holy ground, not daring to see his face, not even daring to touch the ark of the Lord; or hiding in the crack in the rock so as to avoid seeing this holy God face to face. Didn't we have to appease, by penitence and sacrifice, the righteous anger of God at our behaviour? How could our unholiness approach God the Holy High God in whom was no unrighteousness at all? This question keeps on appearing in the Bible. 'I am a man of unclean lips and I live among a people of unclean lips' (Isaiah 6.5).

Behind this question lies the greater problem for monotheism, expressed in a fine book by Austin Farrer: *Love Almighty and Ills Unlimited*. The problem is this: if God is so good, righteous, holy and loving, how come there is so much evil and suffering in the world? This is the single most often recurring question put to believers by those who find the suffering and evil in our world to be a disproof of the existence of God. It is the universal 'why?' It is to this I now turn, not so much trying to answer a question no one else has ever answered, but rather hoping to show how we can believe in a loving, almighty God in the face of earthquake, famine, waste and cruelty, in the terrors and evil which stalk the Earth.

Four

Natural suffering

To stand by a makeshift bed looking at a young mother with
AIDS, clutching a skeletal little baby in her arms, is to feel
there is nothing left to say: all arguments die on the lips. Yet
the doctor standing at the bedside had become a doctor
because his faith in God had called him out of comfort into
risk, and had enabled him to live a life of service and loving
care in dangerous and fraught circumstances. At first sight,
such agonies overwhelm any thought or idea except just to
try doing something. Those involved in such compassionate
action are their own justification, whether believers in God
or not. Yet somehow this first impression is misleading. It
turns out that the beliefs of those patients and doctors are of
paramount importance. One of the patients was convinced
she was being killed by the practice of black magic and, in
addition to her pain and grief, she was also battling with
spiritual terror. She needed to be free of this terror, not only
for her healing but also for her peace of mind. There was also
a young doctor who came to serve but, finding the suffering
and the evil too heavy a weight to carry, having nowhere to
take his feelings of impotence, and having no hope, he
became cynical and defeated. He needed belief in the
possibility of healing and progress to keep him going. The
thoughts we have about evil and suffering, the ideas we have
about God, far from being just abstract ideas, turn out to be
the engine-room of healing and practical care.

We should not then allow the existence of evil and
suffering to stop us thinking and praying, nor just fall back
into the sort of spiritual lethargy which does not have the
drive or the hope or the sense of purpose which mobilizes us

for action. The nearest we get to finding answers is in the struggle, the vision of a better way, and above all in the practical and spiritual love which can transform it. We often shy away from the grief of our world and indeed we can't carry it all, but if we all took on our own particular burden and share of the problem and exercised the gifts we have been given, the world would be changed. But so many people say, 'There is no God', or 'There is no hope', or 'There are no practical steps which can be taken', and as a result adopt the attitude of 'Eat, drink and be merry, for tomorrow we die'. This failure to face up to reality is in itself a sort of neurosis. However understandable it might be, it is a denial of the vocation we all have. If we bury our concern beneath layers of doubt and fear, rather than face it and do something about it, we are running away. It is the acid test of our faith. 'Love must not be a matter of theory or talk. It must be true love which shows itself in action' (1 John 3.18). True religion is not so much a matter of what we say about God, but rather how we live our lives for him, and this in turn depends upon what we believe.

I have often thought that Christian apologists, defending a loving God against the fact of evil and suffering, give the too-easy answer that it is all the fault of the human race. They are so keen to free God from any responsibility: he somehow sits enthroned above it all, having created a garden of Eden, in which there was no pain, no waste, no suffering. According to this interpretation, Adam and Eve rebelled and wrecked the garden, or rather expelled themselves from the garden by their own actions. With that fall, the whole creation fell. This is the danger of stories and parables: they are intended to mean one thing, but can be taken on to mean something else. The story is about the human loss of innocence. The story-teller was describing his understanding that human beings, as distinct from the other animals, want to know more and to become like God. But he also indicated the freedom which God intended to be ours by the exercise of choice. This freedom gave the right to disobey which led to alienation. The consequence was pain and suffering and guilt and exclusion from the garden. Yet it was God who put the tempting tree there in the first place and supplied the serpent.

By their act of disobedience, Adam and Eve became self-conscious and were plunged into the knowledge which increases sorrow.

I believe it reflects that massive evolutionary change from being an innocent, instinctive 'naked ape' to the human being, who had the brain to think and the frightening self-consciousness which brings responsibility and enormous potential: 'they will be like gods'. The story is not intended to show that nature was somehow different in the beginning, free from waste, cruelty and suffering, but rather that a step was taken towards a totally distinctive level of self-consciousness in the human race. The serpent went on its belly and was feared by humans and that's why he was cast in that role of tempter; the woman did have pain in childbirth and the story explained that fact of life by what had happened in her consciousness; and there were thistles and hard ground, resistant to the spade, before man ever discovered how to use one.

When I look at the world, I believe that God must carry ultimate responsibility for its existence and much of its grief. It is a complete denial of his power to say that he created something perfect which turned out to produce evil, waste, cruelty and suffering. God is not some cheap politician who denies responsibility and puts all the blame on the locals. We shall never get anywhere with understanding God unless we accept his ultimate responsibility for the experiment of life itself, and stop blaming human kind for all the bits which go wrong. It seems to me to be clear that from the very beginning of life on the planet, living creatures developed by mutual consumption, by the survival of the fittest, and by a brief cycle followed by death and decay: this was the way God made it, and he is responsible for it. We can't hide from this reality by relying on the idea that somewhere in our prehistory, because of the disobedience of one man, the whole system underwent a universal change in its rule of operation. It was, however, an important and fundamental change for human beings and their effect upon the Earth and on the other creatures because it gave them dominance. In a sense this evolutionary change was another example of what had been happening all along. When the Bible says that by human sin, death came into the world, it is concentrating on human destiny. It is tackling the reality of death, not only at the end of a human life, but the lesser death in the heart of it, day by day.

I remember standing under the statue of a *Tyrannosaurus Rex* in the Natural History Museum, wondering how I could believe in a loving God if he created such a beast, but that was a typical human prejudice. As a friend pointed out, the tyrannosaurus would have looked very beautiful to another tyrannosaurus! At the moment, it is not just theology which is in flight from the cruel reality of a natural order which progresses by predation. Our society also is increasingly adopting an anaesthetized view of the creaturely world. We all have to come to terms with the fact that the rain falls on the just and the unjust, that the wind is not tempered to the shorn lamb, that nature is red in tooth and claw. There is a brute reality which, however fascinating and beautiful it is, is also cruel, wasteful and causes suffering, and we have to accept and live with it. We can't always dash out into the garden of the world trying to save the little bird from the cat ... if we did there would soon be no cats.

When we look death, illness, plague and famine, earth-quake and all forms of natural disaster in the face – let alone the quiet suffering and dying that goes on beneath hedgerow, in drought and flood – we are talking about suffering on a massive scale before we have even reached the point at which human sin breaks on to the scene. To tell the story of creation without pain from the beginning is a theological fantasy. The explosive force of the Big Bang puts violence at source. The Adam and Eve story has a profound significance for us humans without implying that the whole natural world fell into alienation and suffering by their act as well.

Once we admit the possibility of God as ultimately responsible for creation being the way it is, then we have to ask why he could want it to have such capacity for suffering. My thoughts have been affected in these last few days because each morning I have had to walk past a dead sheep, its eyes pecked out by the ravens, its intestines hanging out and its body in rigor. Yet in the field the ewes and the lambs are strong, healthy and enjoying the earth. The sheep died of what are called 'natural causes'. The original 'Earth project' had birth and death built into the plan. Without birth and death, nothing would begin and, even more horrifying, nothing would end. We don't give up planting roses because the flowers will decay and die; rather we plant them because for a brief moment they are a source of beauty and inspiration. We don't give up having pets because we know that they get killed by accidents, because they can suffer from arthritis and are subject to sudden illness. We have pets because the relationship with them and their own reality is intrinsically worthwhile, in spite of the suffering and death which afflicts every living creature. The whole order is in process of becoming and dying, and then becoming the raw material for something else. We have the joy of a baby born into the world but we know it will die, although we hope that before that event it will have flowered like the rose. As the Bible puts it, 'All flesh is grass. The grass withers, the flower fades.'

Some people have found this transience of the creation impossible to accept. The result is that we try too hard to avoid natural death. It was Bertrand Russell who experienced despair because he saw that the Earth itself was transient and would in the end die of cold. He thought that, if all human achievement and creativity came to nothing, this drained life of its purpose. But he had no sense of the dimension of God, of the possibility of there being an eternal purpose. Indeed the Bible is clear that there was a beginning and that there will be an end, an Alpha and an Omega. So transience of nature, including us, is given a new perspective: it becomes part of the process towards eternal life. The conviction that there is this further life, not only has been the most profound comfort to the human heart and mind, but also is essential if there is any ultimate justice in God. As a priest once said in the face of innocent suffering, 'I don't believe in the resurrection; I demand it!'

The question to God, therefore, becomes, 'Could there be a creation without birth, decay and death?' Couldn't God have made it all a bit easier and begun with everlasting life? But how can you begin something that is everlasting? And, if faced with our own life for ever, would we choose it? So much of what we enjoy in our lives and treasure is transient, and I wait to hear the explanation of how everlasting life in the flesh could be anything other than a nightmare. Much of natural suffering comes from this fact of the inbuilt programme of decay and death. If we want to have life then we have to have death. We are as much part of the natural system as that sheep by the road. We may believe that we can accept this reality and recognize that a loving God may have created it.

There are people who will not bring children into the world, because it is such a cruel and sad place. But the fact is that even when there is suffering and risk and pain, the human race goes on reproducing itself. There may be too many children being born, but say there were none, say we lost the will to create children or, as P. D. James described in *The Children of Men*, we lost fertility: human life would decay to its end. Two parents who decide they want to have a child and have the physical capacity to do so, take great risks. They do not know how that child is going to develop. The process of the coming together of one sperm out of millions with one ovum, is a process which, on the surface, is one involving millions of possible children. There is such prodigious waste in the whole system and yet the conception was made in love. The decision, if conscientiously taken, is this: 'We are willing to allow chance on a massive scale to choose one child out of billions of possibilities. We know that there is an outside chance that the child may be seriously handicapped. Even if the child is physically healthy, through the changes and chances of life, through our fault and the fault of the child, or the fault of others, the child may die in tragic circumstances, may become a drug addict, may be unemployable, or become chronically sick and will ultimately die, probably after some years of suffering.' Yet as loving parents many of us take the decision, and it is normally the cause of great joy and lasting satisfaction, with struggles.

Love, therefore, is compatible with a creation which we know will be subject to horrendous risks and can bring grief to us all. We take what steps we can to avoid damaging the child in any way, and try to protect it from danger, but in the end we know that it will have to stand on its own feet, and face up to whatever life throws at it. This risk of giving life is best done out of love and in so doing we demonstrate how we can believe in a God who has done the same on an unimaginably huge scale and has delegated the implementation, but thankfully not abdicated responsibility. If we can decide to bring children into a world with such risks, then God can. We would not have wanted parents who protected us from everything, whether we liked it or not – nor would we want a God who did this.

Before we consider evil and the human contribution to the way the world is, it is important to recognize the ambivalence of nature. People often seem to say, when a tragedy happens, that God should alter the nature of the material world to avoid the suffering in any particular instance. If we consider, however, the elements of our world, they are all ambivalent. From our earliest origins fire has been essential to the human race: as a provider of warmth, as protection against animals, for cooking and later for industrial development. Yet precisely those qualities which make fire helpful to our survival also make it dangerous and potentially lethal. We put a fire on in a room and then spend time trying to teach small children not to go near it. We need the heat, but it brings danger. The same could be said of water without which human life is impossible. We drink it to live, we use it to clean. Stream and river and sea are a great source of power, beauty and recreation, yet precisely those qualities which bring life and pleasure also bring disaster if we can't swim, or we are caught up in flood, or if the water gets out of our control. Or rock, which we rely on to build, to provide stability, which protects us from the energy within the earth itself, and provides copper, coal, gold and diamonds, is the rock which, when it naturally falls from a cliff under the influence of gravity, can kill any innocent creature in its path.

There is this huge ambivalence in the elemental nature of the way things are. Our lives would become impossible to sustain if God could change the character of things in a moment because there was a creature at risk. We would never be able to plan, to have science, to build, even to walk down the street, if things did not obey their inherent qualities as a matter of course. This continues into our own human creativity. We invent and build the motor car. We open up for ourselves enormous possibilities which offer us more experience and freedom of movement, but the car in our hands is also a potential killer. We have invented the flying machine, and it is capable of extending our encounter with the whole world; yet if it loses power, we know it will fall like a stone, and it's no use saying that at that moment we'd like steel to be feathers. There has to be consistent behaviour in the stuff of life or we could not be rational creatures. The DNA profile of every individual may be different, but it consists of the same building blocks and there is an obdurate consistency about the way it works, once we know the rules. In a way this alarming ambivalence of things is one of the facets of being human in which we face the same questions that God faces.

We are described in the Bible as being made in the image of God and that image is, in part, our capacity to create, invent, to extend our capacity, which brings with it terrifying choices. How should we use our harnessing of nuclear power, how develop our genetic engineering, how decide the effects of what we do on the environment?

This is like the challenge in the Book of Genesis when the gods say of Adam and Eve and in the tale of the tower of Babel, 'They will become gods like us' (Genesis 3.5; 11.6). The difficulty is that we often do not see the results of what we do: we are not all-seeing and all-knowing; we make the most terrible mistakes and we distort the ambiguity of the way things are by our greed and pride. In this we are not reflecting the image of God in us. The faith in the goodness of God is a faith which involves the belief that God in his goodness invented the best of all possible worlds, bearing in mind the purpose of his creation. Within that creation, he launches the human experiment of a mind that could share in his creativity, as a free agent, with the ability to choose to do right or wrong – and could strive to know the mind of God.

In *Your God is Too Small*, J. B. Phillips tells a parable. A parent gives his child a balloon. He shows the child how to blow it up, and explains the fun which balloons can bring. He warns the child that if he pricks the balloon or stamps on it, it will burst and will be lost. The child plays with it for a while and then is fascinated by the idea of it bursting, so he stamps on it. The inevitable happens, and the child takes the bedraggled remains to the parent and says, 'mend it.' It's impossible, because of the way it was made and intended to be. When God created the human race he must have known and taken responsibility for what his children would do with the creation he had given them; and believed the experiment to be worthwhile.

The expression 'Almighty God' can be misleading. Almighty cannot mean God can do anything. A God whose overall purpose is love cannot do anything inconsistent with that purpose. We have seen that love emerges from a world fraught with danger and difficulty. There has to be consistency in the way things intrinsically are. This is one of the difficulties about miracles: why does God chose through miracles to 'intrude' upon the way he has created our reality? The answer to this might be that it only seems like an intrusion because we do not see clearly enough the way things really are – especially in the area of the impact of the spiritual on and in the physical world. But as we have also seen, life on Earth is extremely improbable when we consider the nature of the process which brought it to being. Slight variations could damage it or destroy it for ever – and therefore God cannot alter it at will like a tyrant. In this sense God is not 'Almighty'. It would fundamentally undermine the unity of God if he could will ultimate opposites. Out of all the possible worlds the one we have is the one we have been given. God on the Cross reveals the limitation of the power of God on Earth in the pursuit of love and freedom.

We see therefore an extremely risky and dangerous world which the dominant players can make even more dangerous and risky. Belief involves the recognition that God set up this risk and danger as part of the context in which life has to be lived. We may decide that the risk was infinitely worth taking, but it still leaves us with the question as to how an almighty loving God can be involved in it all. Can God be part of the birth, life, decay and death? Religions have taken different routes through this problem. Some have emphasized the distance between God and what he has made. They have taught that change, suffering and decay are features of the cosmos, but God the creator does not change nor suffer and certainly does not decay and die. This distinctiveness of God from what he has made, like the potter with the pot, has the advantage of making God the sublime resting place for the soul, precisely because he is not caught up in the restless painful world. It relies heavily on there being another dimension where God is in his perfection. But that distance can also make God feel like an absentee landlord. He might be pure, holy, unchangeable, but how would he like to be caught up in the mess he has created? This otherness of God can, as we have seen, lead to a view which undervalues the affairs, the attitudes and aspirations of the human race, producing an earth-denying sort of religion which does not get inside the bloodstream of material existence.

Other religions have stressed the involvement of God up to the level of total engagement in the creation, so that the whole cosmic experience is 'engodded'. Here God is seen as sharing in the suffering and ritually going through the seasonal life, decay and rebirth. Hindu teaching, for instance, presents the most radical view of the relationship of God to the mutual devouring which is the basic system in the animal kingdom. It sees a sort of Trinity, not of love, but of the devourer, the devoured and the devouring. This seems very foreign to the Christian view, but it brings the comfort of seeing God as responsible for and indeed involved in the suffering of the natural world. When the wildebeest falls in the clamped jaws of the lion, God is there in the midst of them. This approach has the danger of beginning to equate God with his creation, so that God becomes everything that is, with the accompanying idea that God has no independent life. If God is everything, then maybe God is in reality nothing other than universal reality, and presents us with no morality but our own, no purpose but our own, however much we dress up this totally immersed God in divine aura. Most of the great faiths, including Hinduism, attempt to hold together the 'otherness' of God with his compassionate, merciful engagement with the universe he has created.

Another ambivalence of the natural world, which has

considerable influence on the understanding of God, is the fact of light and darkness. In a way, primitive fear of the dark has given it a bad name. Presumably the night has been a dangerous facet of conscious experience, and we all know how bleak our lives can look on a sleepless night. For many years I was frightened of the dark. The enemy, the one who doesn't like being seen, prowls around seeking whom he may devour! Think of the number of times in religion and in our language that the darkness is seen as the playground of danger and evil. It has certainly played a part in racism, and the Caucasian fear of dark-skinned people. The parables of light and darkness, and the use of darkness as a recurring metaphor for fearful evil, also have a seriously misleading interpretation, as indeed can most parables and metaphors.

It is salutary to gather together some of the positive images of darkness. When you paint, it is shadow that gives the light its meaning and substance. A painting of the natural world without shadow is flat and unreal and uninteresting. I treasure those words from the hymn: 'Through sleep and darkness safely brought, restored to life and power and thought.' Our transient, finite, limited life and energy would be drained away in no time if there were no sleep and darkness, as every insomniac knows. Imagine a natural world that was always under the light of the sun. There would be no dawn and first light touching the gentle hills, no starlit nights, no candle-light, no flickering icons to give us clues to eternity, no rest from seeing and reacting. Just as fear can grow in the dark, so can prayer, because it enables us to concentrate on the invisible. I had the privilege of confirming a young man who was soon to die of AIDS. He had already gone blind and was in darkness. I said to him how terrible it must be not to have his sight, in addition to his other pain and suffering. His reply was this: 'No. I can see all that God wants me to see.' He celebrated his confirmation with a bottle of champagne and then, as he knew would happen, he was violently sick. A few days later he died. The darkness was no threat to him.

There must be primitive and elemental reasons why we identify fear and grief with the dark, because of dangers and death, but without the dark, light has little meaning. As we shall see, there is no goodness without evil, no truth without dishonesty, no purity without impurity. The gift of light is the second gift of God to the universe, according to the Bible, and the first gift was darkness without which the light would have had no meaning.

I have tried in this chapter to show how a believer in God can begin to reconcile the existence of natural suffering, transience, decay and death with the belief that there is an almighty, loving creator. It is important to remember that those who do not believe in God can also be asked for their account of the ways of the natural world. Why is there such consistency in an accidental process? If these people are just an accident within a purposeless, directionless accident, where does their meaning and purpose come from? How do they account for moral and spiritual aspirations, the ideals of the human history, and what grounds do they have for believing in the victory of good? I can admire a sort of stoic acceptance of life contained within the cosmic reality – namely, that we have to make the best of a bad job and do all we can to alleviate the pain and suffering. But where did we get this nobility from, and why should evil not triumph in a continuing accidental process? It is not my intention to try to undermine the beliefs that sustain others, but at least in the severe critique of religion and faith in God which is the persistent view expressed by the 'cultured despisers', it seems right to point out that the unanswered questions, the mystery at the heart of the spirit, and the search for meaning remain part of their problem too. Cynicism, hedonism and materialism are no answer to the yearning of the human soul, and to me that very yearning suggests the divine origin of the universe in which we live.

Having considered the question of natural suffering I now want to move on to consider the reality of evil and the human part in the cause of suffering.

Five

What is it to be human?

This is another of those ancient and modern questions. It's not only 'what does it mean to be a member of the human race?', but also 'what does it mean to be me?' The fact that we constantly wonder about these questions is one of the ways in which we differ from the rest of the natural world. Leopards, as far as we know, do not ask what it means to be a leopard, nor what it means to be that particular leopard. An eagle does not, as far we know, ask itself, as it soars over mountains, 'Why am I here, and how do I fly, and who am I?' Yet we bear strong resemblance to the natural world of which we are part, and share many characteristics of the animal kingdom: we recognize the desire to mate and reproduce; we show aggression and contentment; we know thirst and hunger; we experience fear and the will to survive; we need territory and often demonstrate a herd instinct. We share some key foundation qualities and many of the same experiences, but we also have qualities, abilities and fundamental attitudes which set us apart.

Human beings have much in common with the animal kingdom but they are also essentially different from it. I think that close observation of the natural world and its increased visual accessibility to people through the media are very important education for the survival of life on earth. But seeing the natural world on television is different from living or working, or sharing habitat with animals. For most of us, our closest view of animals is through our pets. There we see loyalty, affection, a sense of fun, a shrewdness. Although some of these qualities come from their basic instincts, much derives from their training and conditioning by the close

association with humans. The use of rewards and punish-
ments, the giving and withdrawing of affection as a control
factor, enable us to develop the acceptable side of the
animal's character, but it is normally at the cost of its
freedom. Woe betide a domestic animal if, after this
conditioning, we release it into the wild or if it reverts to
wild behaviour in our home. Part of our problem is that we
project onto animals the feelings and thoughts we develop
through our pets, and this can cause us to make serious
ecological mistakes. The fact is that animals are for the most
part instinctive creatures who have a direct response to any
experience of fear, hunger, pain, reproduction, urge for
territory, without being troubled by moral, intellectual
questions, without the imagination which is both the bane
and the beauty of the human race.

The animals are innocent, because sin can only derive
from moral consciousness and knowledge. A stag in the rut
gathers together as many hinds as he can win by battling with
other stags. He doesn't think, 'I was really beastly to that
young stag', whereas human beings (well, most of us) would
be asking ourselves whether this was the right way to treat
people. If there are weak or disabled members of the tribe,
human beings worry, or at least feel they ought to worry,
that they should have done something to help. Before any
important event, a man or woman or child can go through
endless possible scenarios in their minds, with eager
anticipation or dread. Animals, on the other hand, respond
to the immediate, or what they have come to expect by
habit.

When we look at the ceiling of the Sistine chapel, we
know that it was created by an imaginative and vulnerable
human mind, using all its instinctive gifts of sight, feeling and
touch. They are tools in the mind of the master artists, and
can be an expression of the person he has become, a portrayal
of where his soul has journeyed and what he believes. But it
is not only the peaks of human achievement which
demonstrate this distinctive humanness, but also the pit.
When we consider Auschwitz, or the damage done by the
bomb dropped on Hiroshima, we see all the human skills and
experience being used for massively wicked and destructive

acts, which are possible precisely because of the capacities which distinguish the human from the animal. They distort or transcend the instincts by evil imagination, wickedness or technical brilliance.

Human beings also have a far greater capacity to acquire, store, process, communicate and use information. We can solve problems by behaviour and decision rather than by evolution alone. Our species has, for a very short time, inhabited a tiny speck in an inconceivably vast universe and in our minuscule lifetime, the human mind aided by its developing technology has gone on 'Star Trek'. Small birds migrate thousands of miles each year but their consciousness, their instincts, are tied to each moment.

So, we have a problem. We see this problem writ large in war, in national and international affairs. Society multiplies the individual sin by pooling its effect. This allows the individual to hide behind the corporate identity and escape responsibility. We shall look at this later. We also recognize the ambivalence in ourselves. The problem and the potential is found in us. We know that we are all a mixture of the good and the bad. As soon as we developed from being simply instinctive creatures to being self-conscious, thinking humans, we plunged into infinite questions. We struggle in our attempt to be what others want us to be and it's even harder to be what we want ourselves to be. Any realistic view of our lives confronts us with the hurt and damage we have done to ourselves and to others. We may exaggerate the harm we have done and get it out of proportion, or we may underestimate it, or not even realize how wrong we have been, but a conservative estimate leads almost all of us to recognize that we have sinned and been sinned against. It may be just the usual mild mess that goes on in our lives. I have never met anyone who has done no wrong, and I have met a great many people who have done serious wrong.

We know that there is a vast amount of human goodness in the world. However, when we add together all human wrongdoing, its short and long term effects, its multiplication in society, it is not hard to see how much of the suffering in the world is caused by human sin. If we were to add up in the

United Kingdom the suffering caused to children by marriage breakdown and divorce; or calculate the suffering caused in the hungry or starving two-thirds of the world by our corporate selfishness and greed; or assess the fear, injury and death created by violence and war; or the emotional pain caused by dishonesty and cruelty in human relationships; or the disasters caused by carelessness or irresponsibility; or the illness caused by promiscuity and sexual infidelity; or the hurt and conflict caused by hate or racism or bigotry; or the harm done to our environment and atmosphere .... The pain, damage and suffering is vast and we all share in it to more or less an extent. Therefore, even when we have taken account of the suffering in the world caused by its nature, by the way it is, we have also to recognize the vast scope of the suffering caused by human folly or sin.

Conscience is therefore at the heart of what it means to be human. To encounter those who have no conscience left is a terrifying experience. On the other hand I have also encountered people who have an obsessive sense of their own guilt, sometimes completely unrelated to the facts of the case. Both conditions are intensely dehumanizing. The alienation and danger of the psychopath, and the despair of someone obsessed by imagined or distorted guilt, serve to remind us how precious and central a good conscience is to our humanity and sanity. Because of the evil and suffering which can be caused by the human race, conscience is closely linked to the problem of suffering and evil in the world. This 'moral law within' is a matter with which religion is acutely concerned. Yet the conscience is often neglected or misunderstood.

Conscience has been defined as 'the human mind making moral judgements'. It is not a substance although it is intensely related to the whole person and especially dependent on the operation of the brain. It appears to operate in two main ways. The conscience tells us what we should or should not do. It then judges or commends us for what we have done, or not done. It is one of the essential triggers of our personality. Its guidance and monitoring of our behaviour has a great deal to do with the person we become. Unless there is some severe disability or brain damage, the potential is there for every human being to have a conscience.

When we evaluate another person, a large element of the assessment is based upon how we think that person's conscience is operating. We might say to ourselves that he or she is a thoroughly unpleasant character, insensitive, rude and selfish. If you think about the people you know well, your criticism arises either because of particular actions or because of their habitual frame of mind. Even in the petty matters of life, like paying for a round of drinks, we judge someone who always ducks out of their round if we know they can well afford to pay their share. We make a judgement about their personality on the basis of the non-operation of their conscience. We have a whole range of such judgements of people who lie and deceive others, people who steal or are violent and abusive, people who look down on others and are snobs, people who couldn't care less about suffering going on around them.

We also make positive judgements when we think a person's conscience works well: 'You can always rely on her'. 'He has a marvellous sense of humour, but he's never cruel with it.' Our evaluation of other people is often based upon the way a person's conscience operates, for good or ill. As we get to know people better we may begin to make allowances. We may find out that they have had an appalling family background, or been through some tragic experiences, or just been seriously disadvantaged in their lives. We begin to see why they are as they are. We may recognize that there is some mental or psychological illness or disability which has resulted in the conscience malfunctioning or being undeveloped. Although these serious facts have to be taken into account, if we say a person has no responsibility, we deprive them of their identity.

One of the recurring, public arguments about responsibility, in its simplest form, says that because a person lives in degrading circumstances, or poor environment, or has been abused, then they are not responsible for their actions. In my experience there is a lot of truth in this, but I have never believed that it deprived a person of their own conscience. Somehow when you say that a person cannot be blamed for wickedness, you are denying that person's humanity in a fundamental way. The next step may be not to expect any goodness to emerge from that source. People, for instance, talk about certain housing estates as if living there deprived people of virtue and responsibility, yet we know that there are people in each place who are holy and heroic in the way they have coped. There is often a right judgement against society for allowing such a damaging environment to exist, but the individuals still keep responsibility for their conscience. Only in such a way will they keep their human dignity. Making allowances is important but, if carried too far, it can degrade the person. By our law we recognize the limited responsibility of a child for its actions, but he/she still carries a child's degree of moral identity. There is a useful old adage that 'ought implies can': that is to say, you can only be morally responsible for what you are capable of knowing and doing. But to have no capacity to respond at any level is to deny our humanity.

The conscience may be damaged or whole; it may be asleep or awake; it may be well informed or ignorant; it may be tender or hard. It is the mind of a person making moral judgements, and therefore will depend on both the nature of the person and their nurture. That is, it will depend upon the intrinsic character as well as the attitudes and behaviour patterns developed by experience. Children in the same family will often display amazingly different characteristics yet operate according to the general standards of their family or grouping. There are, of course, many extreme experiences which can break up the normal pattern, both in terms of the individual character and the way in which the norms of a family affect different members. For instance, an extrovert family lifestyle may be a pain to an introverted child. Or being an only child may push him or her into a withdrawn way of life, or into desperate attempts to win the affection of others.

It's important to recognize that there are views about the human race which see conscience itself as an illusion, which doubt that any sense of altruism may survive if it exists at all. 'The selfish gene rules.' But such arguments seem themselves, in the name of the genetic, to fly in the face of a large part of reality and minimize the aspect of the human race which is spiritual. There is much in our innermost being which is assertive, selfish, uncaring but it looks hopelessly near-sighted to ignore all that is in us which has given us faith in an individual soul – a soul made to love.

I am convinced that the greatest influence on the development of a person is the personal environment in which they grow up. Once I was waiting in a London hospital to see a consultant. On either side of me was a parent and each had a small child. The one parent spent the whole time we were waiting playing with the child and allowing the child to cuddle and climb and talk and laugh, and anyone could see the intimate nature of the relationship. The other parent had a mobile phone and spent the whole waiting period talking to friends in a loud voice. This parent had to smack the child a dozen times for misbehaving which was mostly because the child was curious and bored. It was not just the continuous smacking which jarred, but the words that went with it.

For the first child the wait was a lovely intimate time with his father who was obviously a poor Bangladeshi. For the second child it was a time of frustration and alienation from its mother. This real-life parable is not just about poverty but also about poverty of relationships which can obviously happen in situations where the people are well-off. When you see a child in a school class who is totally withdrawn, disturbed, or violent, you can usually guess that the trouble begins at home. It is not inevitable that poverty of home circumstances will make the love deteriorate, but it does put the parents under great added pressure and stress. The development of conscience is both a matter of nurture and nature, and is a main key to personal identity. It is the factor that has more to do with personal satisfaction and happiness than any other. It is a function, an expression of the whole self we are becoming.

But is this conscience a law to itself? Is it just an individual matter? How much ought we to take in external authority? This emerges sometimes at a very early period of our lives when young children reject the moral guidance of their parents and their teachers. Of course there has always been teenage rebellion but there seems to be a new level of independence and rejection of adult guidance. When I grew up there were sanctions and, if we rebelled, the trick was not to be found out. Whereas now, more and more children not only reject parental and teacher authority, but are willing to face it out. There are real dangers here which may have a long-term damaging effect as well as the indiscipline of the immediate moment. It gives a great deal more power to the peer group and the media. Moral attitudes begin to be derived more from friends and role models in the soaps and the teenage world than from the elders of their own family and community. This tends to emphasize the individuality of conscience and the claiming of moral authority, even when the person's experience and understanding are still minimal. The conscience needs teaching and illuminating and for years may have to accept external authority on major issues.

Again, it is not difficult to see how this development has happened. The 'Rebel Without a Cause' rejected the poor relationships and empty values of a materialistic, selfish and hidebound society. He was not 'without a cause!' Part of the sympathy we had for him was because his parents were so blind to their own lack of moral vision. James Dean came to symbolize the youthful desire for freedom from the poverty of the adult understanding of life. But the rebel can become disconnected from what should be usefully passed on from generation to generation. A child can be making moral judgements without a proper frame of reference before he/she is ready for the degree of independence. We saw this happen with exceptional severity in the West Indian and Bangladeshi communities who came to East London in the 1950s and 1960s. In encountering the white liberal society, the children of immigrants often broke away from the norms and restraints of their parents' culture, and rejected the authority of their elders who found that they had none of their usual sanctions in their new social setting. This was more than the normal rebellion of the younger generation. It often could not be contained within the rituals of growing up under the shelter and protection of their parents. It often led to a serious alienation and revealed how important this maturing process is. It also showed how significant for the inner conscience the understanding of parental or adult authority can be. If somehow the adult authority is lost altogether, then personal anarchy can quickly follow. Of course there is often profound need for change because of cultural turmoil, but the damage derives from the ultimate breakdown of trust. There are parents who themselves cause this breakdown by their own behaviour and they will have been responsible for this fracture of the mind, but sometimes it is because they too have been overwhelmed by cultural tides which have been almost impossible to resist. It is not surprising that the clash is often expressed in terms of religious attitudes because religion is closely involved, both with moral formation and authority.

The teaching of children in faith and morality is recognized by all religions as highly important. It is significant that even in our highly secularized society, the large majority of parents still believe that such instruction is important. So it is that most children in the UK receive some basic instruction about the various religions available. I am sure this helps in terms of reducing prejudice and creating a better level of understanding. It fits too comfortably, however, with the supermarket approach to life. You look at what's on the shelf and take what you want. There are other profound weaknesses in this approach because it is not always possible to find teachers for whom any of these religions are a central or important aspect of their lives (just as the majority of children grow up in families where religion is rather like a remote insurance policy kept in the file until a claim has to be made or a small premium paid). It is certainly possible to teach about religion as one subject among others but it is unlikely that such teaching will make any effective inroads into the personality of a child without the encouragement, the commitment of people for whom faith is essential to their lives. The basic responsibility for this must lie with the parents first and then the church. Faith and morality cannot truthfully be taught without the personal love and commitment of those who themselves love God.

I cannot help but feel that many parents of my generation have let our children down because we believed that we should not indoctrinate them. We thought that we should allow them to make their own choices in the sphere of religion and morality before they were ready. This social and cultural pressure discouraged the direct and committed teaching of the faith. Our less direct approach had its own strengths, because it encouraged an open mind and avoided the dehumanizing results of too much religion. It is distressing to meet a child, brought up in a religious hothouse or strait-jacket, who has never been able to have a full and free engagement with childhood. But, just because we see the dangers of sectarian religion, we should not think that there are no ways of sharing our faith with our children. This would indeed be to surrender to the spirit of the age and I think it has resulted in the stream of religious vision going underground. We can still see the fruits of this vision influencing the beliefs and morality of our children but the springs are subconscious and largely unrecognized. It's rather like the effect of the water-table on the growth of the vegetation above, because the roots are reaching down to the hidden springs. But then comes the question: how can this hidden spring come to the surface when there is such a huge weight of secular concrete at ground level?

The older generation are left feeling that they believe the love of God lies at the heart of what is important in life, but they grieve that for their children this spring is submerged in a deep well with a lid fixed in place. There is so much in the world which appears to confirm the children's view that religion is a thing of the past and irrelevant to their lives. It sometimes feels like a battle we've lost before it has begun. But we need to hang in there, to recognize the just criticisms of religion, and yet in a steady way not be afraid to show our own dependence on God, and wait. So many of our fears come from the fact that we believe our God is too small. When we look at the way that young people brought up during the repression of religion in communist countries are now seeking passionately for what they have missed, when we see the search for something more than materialism which is already drawing many young people in society to look for God, the 'elders' should not be impatient.

The younger generation have so much to offer the elders. Every generation of elders thinks that the younger generation is missing out, but if God is real and if they are God's children, he has the power to make the springs within them bubble up to the surface. I am encouraged that it is often the children who lead their parents by the hand back to God. It is moving to see sceptical parents being gently opened up both by the faith of their children and by their own sense of parental responsibility. Almost concealed behind the smoke-screen of their children's interest, they discover something profound starting to happen. The gate of their spirit edges open, and they allow their imagination as children of God to work.

The conscience remains one of the ways by which people can discover the springs of God that lie within themselves. We all have moral perceptions and attitudes. Only the cynic can say that our conscience is unimportant. Most people can recognize, when they think about such things, that they want to be morally serious human beings. We recognize within ourselves a person who wants to do right and does not want to do wrong. On this precious faculty depends the future of society. It must not be allowed to stagnate, or be buried under hedonistic attitudes, or be killed off by the mockery and cynicism of the age. Inside this 'moral law within' can be found a door into relationship with God.

It's important to explore our conscience, not in the sense of looking at the bad old videos in the mind store, but rather to look into that conversation inside ourselves which wrestles with right and wrong, which carries our self-assessment, both when the verdict brings satisfaction and when it leaves a negative or even bad feeling. But if we examine that familiar place, we shall find that our self-assessment is not just based on what we do for others. It's also about the way we see and understand ourselves, in our whole personality. We are concerned about the sort of person we are and are becoming. For the atheist or humanist, this is worked out entirely within a human framework. There is strength there in the sense that if the conscience is active and sensitive, there will be a proper concentration on the human beings involved, on both ourselves as well as others. In some people this can lead to a highly moral and concerned way of life, and I have frequently encountered such people who in practical terms often do what we should also expect of Christian people. But I do not believe that they have discovered the fullness of life they would discover if their minds were opened up to God. I've often thought that if such a person could only discover God they would be even more wonderful. I believe, however, that in this exploration of the person I am, in the search of what conscience means to my identity, I discover something other than, or beyond, myself, which is ever distinct from and beyond relationships with other people.

Some people say, in musing about the existence of God, 'I believe there's something, someone, out there.' But they don't go on to give 'It' a name. We see in Somerset a stream of people, from the New Age Travellers to the quiet truth seekers, who are looking for clues to that 'someone out there'. A young man who wrote to me recently said this: 'I believe strongly in a creator to everything, whether this force be God or Allah. I don't understand how Jesus is the Son of God. I believe he was, like Mohammed and Abraham, a prophet spreading love and forgiveness. With so much corruption in organized religion, I have taken shelter in my own personal belief and strive to be loving, honest and patient.' They are like people of every age who are on a personal pilgrimage, gently swimming with the undercurrent of something within them, which is beyond what they can define or confine.

This is important, not only for our personal integrity, but also for our world. We need a mighty army of just, good, conscience-guided people if we are to tackle the injustice in the world – the hunger, the homelessness, the unemployment.

This is for many people a starting point in their search for God but the search is quickly, for most, put away in a cupboard. Life is, after all, too short to explore such matters in any depth! The result is that many intelligent people get on with the rest of their lives and leave this 'something/someone out there' as a vague idea, perhaps even as a set of clichés, with which they have to make do until a child reminds them of the questions they once asked. It can be some terrible or beautiful event in their lives which bursts through the shell and penetrates the secular concrete of unknowing. If we are looking for a car or a job, or a house, or take a holiday, or plan the garden or plough a field, we think and work out the details of what we want to achieve, and which is the best way to do it. We want to know what is the best deal, before we invest ourselves in it. But, somehow, the spirit of the age has convinced the majority of people that it's not really necessary to explore God. We can make do with only the smallest enquiry. Yet, ultimately, what could be as important as this question of the 'something out there'? Belief in that would affect all the rest. It's rather like living by the side of a mountain and never wanting to climb it or explore the view from the top.

In our inner conversations we constantly weigh ourselves up. We constantly talk to ourselves, ponder in the long reaches of the night, going over things again and again. 'I should never have said that, how could I have been so cruel?' 'What a wonderful day . . . I'd be happy to stay here for ever.' 'I'll never get it right, everything I say seems to make it worse.' 'What if the tests are positive?' 'I'll never forgive him.' 'How could I betray her like that?' 'God, I'm depressed; nobody wants me . . . they think I'm too young, too old, too short, too tall, too inexperienced, too loud-mouthed, too quiet, too over-the-top, too repressed' . . . and so on.

This is the nature of much of our inner life. Brian Keenan wrote a classic of our age about his experience of being a hostage in *An Evil Cradling*. In a way it's not surprising that some of the most profound books about the spirit have been written in prison or after it, because they derive from the fiercest concentration of thought. The book is not only about his personal suffering, nor just about those trapped with him, but it's also about illumination of the inner self. He later described it as being opened to an 'immensity' in himself. This experience was, and still is, deep spiritual surgery.

However, we don't have to go to prison to explore the 'immensity' in ourselves. Thank God most of us don't end up as hostages, though we all know milder forms of imprisonment. We all experience being trapped in situations:

with particular people, or perhaps, worst of all, in the prisons we create round our own heart. Freedom remains one of the greatest yearnings of the human being.

In this inner conversation, in this largely discrete world of ours, in this reflection on our lives, we can discover a 'you' which is distinct from us and is addressable by us. This discovery is a turning-point. We then realize that we are not alone in the inner self. When we feel we can identify this 'you' in us, this 'someone' intimate and yet more than myself, we are being opened up to an immensity of spirit within us. It can be an intensely personal discovery, not necessarily in a big and dramatic moment, but also stealing on the inward ear through a thousand thousand little moments. Although I can identify the time when I fell hook, line and sinker for God, I find it more difficult to be clear about all the personal preparation for that moment. Where were the roots of this clear idea that there was a 'you' in me? Perhaps it was in worship as a child, or walking in a wood at dusk and seeing a great stag raise his head to look, or perhaps in drawing on some source of courage to cope with two bullies who used to harass me on the way home from school, or perhaps it was in the continuous and steadfast love of my parents and my sister, or perhaps it was swimming in the clear ocean, or reaching the summit of a mountain, or meeting and being cherished by certain good and holy people, or perhaps being part of a great football crowd, or seeing a racehorse stretch over the fences at Cheltenham or perhaps it was .... Within the living of a very ordinary life, this conviction grew that there was 'someone there' who was greater than myself and an immensity I could explore.

For a long time this conviction was just a vague idea, more like an excitement or a presence or a hope. It was the deliberate search for knowledge and a deeper relationship with this 'you' (or 'Thou') which step by step took me to believe in God. I was persistent in my search because I sensed how important it was for me. I was even helped by the desperate feelings I had about much of my life in my late teens and early twenties. These were also a big block because I was afraid that the God I was discovering was the invention of my need, as Freud and others had suggested; but I learnt that what I discovered was all so much greater than my own invention. I began to see that some of my atheist friends were rejecting God because of their needs. I also learnt that need is the way we learn to eat and drink and love and hope and trust, and as natural and proper a route to truth as academic study.

It always interests me when people say that when someone they love has died, they talk to them. 'I know he's there.' Of course it's easy to write this off as a comfortable illusion, a continuation in the mind of the nice feelings we had about the person when they were alive, like a replay of old tapes. It's not like that for the people themselves, however, who have a real sense of the presence of their loved one. I've never been able to do this myself. Although I sometimes talk to my mother and father, and particular friends as if they were there because I believe in heaven, I can't feel they are here in the same way as I feel God is. Yet I recognize this form of conversation with a 'Thou'. It's often associated with a long-term relationship which has been interrupted by death, such as a son to a parent or a long-married husband and wife. I have come to believe that something eternal can break through into this life where love is concerned.

I find it helpful to remember that both Jesus and Paul spoke to this 'Thou' in their lives with the word 'Abba'. The nearest translation is the word 'Dad'. It is a word a Jewish child might use for his or her father. God is an intimate 'Thou' for us all ... but that is to leap ahead.

The emergence of the human race on the earth has brought the possibility of good and evil. Part of this evil derives from the struggle to progress from animal innocence to human self-consciousness. The moral choice which we have increases the suffering and introduces sin which is the conscious doing of wrong or the failure to do right. At the heart of this struggle is the conscience. The conscience evaluates ourselves and others, and is the lifeline of the good and the right and the just in our world. We need to reflect upon it, and sharpen its perceptions. It must not be permanently asleep or inactive or blind but informed and sensitive. There is a vast task to tackle the evil and suffering in the world.

In this reflecting on our conscience, the realization can dawn that there is 'someone there' who cares for us, makes demands on us, forgives us and even loves us. When it happens, it is a transforming experience. Although it can make us feel unworthy and even guilty, it also can bring a sense of enormous well-being and assurance. It means that we are not fundamentally alone. Our longing for love is not an illusion, but the saving appetite. We know from our conscience that it is not just what we do that can damage us and others but what we think and feel as well. This too can harm our inner self and cause hurt beyond ourselves. Somehow the thoughts we have as individuals can pour into a spirit of the age, or to fashions and attitudes, and so influence what society becomes. The good conscience is an invisible spiritual strength, a sort of boost to the positive vibes. The bad in us can be like some sort of spiritual pollution. It can only be measured by its indirect results – by the depression, despair and even depravity in society – like acid rain. The lust for money, the culture of envy, racial bigotry, do not feed just on what people do but on what they think and feel. So our human minds, making moral judgements, have to deal with the bad and the good. The conscience affirms those things which satisfy, bring hope and peace and strength, and are founded on love; and denies what is harmful, degrading, cruel and covetous.

I have tried to describe a growing recognition of the 'someone there' in our hearts and minds – the 'Thou' of our experience as emerging from this inward conversation. If we explore and perhaps even search for this 'One' who keeps intimate company with us, we grow in the love and vision and praise which express our growing adoration of God. Behind all the tangles, the muddle and confusion, the fun, the joys and the distress, the laughter and the pain of our story, there is this continuous other consciousness, with whom we are relating. This other being assesses, affirms, denies, encourages, judges and forgives us. Increasingly we come to believe that this 'Thou' in our lives is the same 'Thou' that my brother and sister experience, and the same 'Thou' that the universe experiences. No wonder it's a big issue.

Six

Birth and death

It seems important to take these two facts of life together. Birth is a step into being. It is a step from the unknown to the known. Death on the other hand is a step from what we have known and begun to understand, back into the unknown.

If we think of the process of conception, gestation and birth, it is profoundly puzzling to imagine how our identity develops in that journey. What happens is such a mixture of the relationship between our parents and their genetic history, in a physical process where the odds are stacked against any winning combination. All those millions of potential human beings battle to live and somehow, in the flow, a person starts to develop. Scientists can increasingly describe what is happening physically but spiritually it remains a mystery. It certainly looks like a matter of chance that we were the identikit which was born. In this process we are like the rest of nature where chance plays such an important part in reproduction. But our blessed affliction of self-consciousness makes us want to understand and discover how our identity came to be. By the study of genetics we understand more about the way our potential is built into a particular initial foetus, but then our minds stumble as we try to trace the path to the incredibly complex human being we become. It remains one of those amazing mysteries that something emerging from so much chance should give rise to a creature so consumed with the need for identity. Is this need also our way in to a god who fills the gaps, or is it a powerful sign that God created us?

An overwhelming experience of birth for the parents is

that their baby has its own unique personality and must be given a name. It's not surprising that new mothers and fathers often experience at this moment what they come to see as religious feelings. As they hold their baby, there is a sense of wonder at something greater than they are, yet somehow still timeless. This glimpse of joy can be the trigger for many a search for God. As the child grows from birthday to birthday, to be a teenager and then an adult, it's a stunning thought to ponder the growth of independence and individuality from such a conception. For me one of the greatest expressions of this wonder comes from an ancient song, where the writer sees this process as profoundly the work of God. 'You it was who fashioned my inward parts; you knitted me together in my mother's womb. My body was no mystery to you when I was formed, woven in the depths of the Earth' (Psalm 139 vv. 13, 15).

The fundamental conviction that there is a 'Thou' in our lives transforms the way we look at life from birth to death. This emergence of a human being, within and as a result of this struggling together of male and female, the desire, sweat and love combining two people in one, cannot be defined or rationalized away. To do so would be to deprive us of one of the greatest sources of our own character and drama, and ultimately drain our destiny of any meaning. But it is a messy business. I always remember the slight look of distaste of the obstetrician who guided our slithery children from the womb. For him who had done a thousand such deliveries, it was still a miracle, but a rather messy one. But there's something wonderful about it all that restores to life a new impetus and hope and possibility. That's why it is so harsh and deep a pain when it goes wrong, or when the possibility is lost altogether. Birth is potentially a precious gathering and pooling of love and joy, yet women often go through the process as victims and their child may be a future victim of loveless or impossible relationships.

I have never forgotten the young girl I know who had her dead baby in secret because of her fears. She wrapped him in a brown paper parcel and hid him in a cupboard. She bore it all alone in terror and bloody sweat and the miracle was stillborn. It's not surprising that the church continues to persuade people that this process of birth must be undertaken within the security of loving and faithful relationship, and reminds us of the responsibility and joy it should bring. Birth is a risky business for the future person even if the process itself has been made so much safer as a result of medical science. The step from the unknown into the world is one which raises the question of God because of the huge sense of responsibility for this unique new human being which it brings.

But what about the other end of our earthly life? Birth and death to my mind need to be thought about together if we are looking for the meaning and purpose of the human experience. From the unselfconscious conception, through birth and growth, through our adult lives, we build a personality to which we have contributed our years. At birth, any identity is given in the genes or in the love or lack of love of those involved with the birth and care of the baby, but when we come to death, we are ourselves. We are the result of our own story with its mistakes, its sins, its goodness, its courage, its cowardice, its love and its hate. We can look back over our years and replay the tapes of what we have seen and experienced. Some events have been of great significance and millions have almost no significance at all, but it all adds up to a person. We know how important memory is to our identity. We recognize when the power to remember is distorted or lost altogether that the identity is irreparably damaged on this earth at least. But for most of us the flower fades, the engine coughs and splutters, we don't function physically so well and we head for death. Experience suggests that the person we have been in the mainstream of our life moulds the person we become as we grow old. To grow old, full of grace, is an art form, and a great deal depends upon the way our personality and our spirit have developed beforehand. Life does not fall into neat and separate compartments; we reap what we sow, whether it be the hardened spiritual arteries of selfishness and bitterness, or the peace and acceptance of a life lived in harmony with the self we have the potential to be. For all of us it's a mixture of good and bad which forms the profile – the CV with which we contemplate death – the further step into the unknown.

Consider Hamlet's encounter at the grave with the skull of poor Yorick. The remains of the person, whom Hamlet had known well, is there in the earth. It is soon decayed and reduced to bone. Hamlet looks at the skull as if it was a mirror. It was a time of renaissance of the human spirit, bringing hope after the long winter of a death-dominated Middle Ages. Even that time of confidence in the human adventure suffered the ultimate threat to its self-sufficiency. Shakespeare wrote:

> What a piece of work is man! how noble in reason! how infinite in faculty! in form and moving how express and admirable! in action how like an angel! in apprehension how like a god! the beauty of the world! the paragon of animals! And yet, to me, what is this quintessence of dust? man delights not me. (*Hamlet*, Act II, Scene II)

In the end we are in physical terms a 'quintessence of dust'. We all have to be born and journey to the other essential, death. In our Cathedral at Wells, Bishop Beckynton's tomb (1466) shows both the great bishop lying in state with the grandeur of his beautiful robes and his power and authority, but also he is represented underneath as a skeleton, naked bone, a quintessence of dust. He built this tomb before he died to remind everyone that we share a common fate and that there is no escape from it. The valley of the shadow of death was ever present. It is perhaps the most striking difference between their age and ours. They lived with the ever-present threat of death whereas, in our society, we have pushed death further and further into its own corner. We hear about, and may even experience, a young death in our family or friends, but it is very much the exception in the affluent West. For those who live in some parts of Africa death is all around them and hunger and disease claims young and old. It can become so commonplace, like sparrows dead by the roadside.

When you explore past civilizations, you soon realize that they wanted a map of their destiny after death. Etruscan tombs are guarded by a leopard painted over the entrance and a burial chamber decorated with deer and the beauty of the natural world. The Pyramids revealed the pharaoh in the grave surrounded by his wealth and favourite wives. The tombs in our churches and cathedrals are often surrounded by angels and archangels. Many of the Tudor tombs show the husband and wife, with their dog at their feet, and their children, several having predeceased them, lined up in prayer, in no doubt as to their destiny in heaven. Through the ages, the wealthy and powerful who could afford tombs have concentrated not just on their achievements but also their destination with God. But alongside this vision of the after-life came the question of the final judgement. Dante used the picture of paradise and hell to confront the powerful people of his day with their ultimate fate before God ... naming names. The Viking warrior was dressed in his full splendour, laid in state upon his boat, set alight and cast out to sea in his flaming bier as he entered Valhalla, the hall of the brave. In so many ways, human beings have described the after-life, and its threat or promise has been for many the strongest motivation to good behaviour in this life.

Our own generation treat death very differently. After the Victorian obsession with it, we evade it. Through two World Wars and the Holocaust, the crumbling in the secular mind of any idea of the after-life, the collapse and disappearance of heaven and hell, death has become almost entirely just a human experience. I could never get over the twelve minutes we were allowed for a cremation service in London. It was like a queue for nothing in particular. There was not time to tell the person's story, no time to grieve. Just when the identity was all-important the system reduced it to a brief disposal. Important memories and feelings have to be shared and mutual support given. But so often the whole event, and the bereavement which follows, carry no picture of what death itself entails and rarely convey any sense of an eternal destiny as the climax and goal of our lives. We have exchanged a vision of eternal life for a few worn-out clichés and the desire to deal with the death as simply and as quickly as possible.

To be obsessed with death, like the Victorians, seems to me to be an error and can be a denial of the importance of this life. To reduce it, however, to a grey exit, or even to try to ignore it, and certainly to have no way of thinking about it, and to pretend that it won't happen to us, is a sort of modern neurosis. Because we have no framework of belief about the after-life, we cannot give death any positive meaning apart from a person's release from a life no longer worth living. A neurosis is a refusal to face up to reality. Perhaps those who are content with the dust and ashes believe that they are the realistic ones, because they think there is nothing awaiting us and it's best to pass it by with as little fuss as possible; but for me it is a denial of so much in the eternal dimension which is important for the human destiny. Because we are afraid to contemplate death, we remove from life an awareness of what is intensely human and precious. A signpost to nothing does not encourage enthusiastic walking!

Death can seem so remote from children, almost as though they were immortal, and in a way that's right. In today's world they already have to grow up far too quickly. My greater concern is that they are faced every day with images of death on film and television. In almost any hour of the day, people are being blasted away, hurling backwards from the force of the bullet, crashing through breaking glass, falling from great heights. The television road accident warnings are themselves intentionally terrifying as another child is thrown up onto the bonnet of a car. The video games have as their main feature the zapping of people in conflict. Of course, children have long been playing games involving simulated violence and death in their imagination, even if they didn't have such realistic toys and access to such repeated images of death. It is of real concern, however, what such a constant confrontation with death in the moving image does to the person's ability to cope with death itself. It's made worse when we offer no interpretation of what death itself might mean. How do we answer the child's question about what happens to us when we die? I suspect that we either find some way to avoid the question or produce some answer from our childhood faith which no longer sustains us, like 'He's gone to be with Jesus' (which I believe to be true, but which usually lacks the ring of truth).

In some people this failure to think through what death

means to us leads to a morbid curiosity about death, gathering every detail. For others it results in flight from the fear of death and a total avoidance of its associations. For others 'eat, drink and be merry' has to provide the evasion. But however much we try to hide from it, run away from it, anaesthetize ourselves against it, death happens to us and to those we love. At some time our brains stop and our bodies come to a halt. Like birth it is essential to being human. This threat of nil further experience – no flicker on the monitor – is a major fact about our lives and on the whole we ignore it as though it is irrelevant until sometime in the remote future when it will happen to us.

I was saddened by the death of a young man in an air crash. Most of the people at the funeral were young and, as business people in the 1980s, they had the appearance of Yuppies, as they were called in those days. They appeared to be full-blast focused on their splendid lives, smartly dressed, fully geared up, and to all appearances greatly successful. Then suddenly, in the midst of this splendour, they were confronted with the death of their young friend and inwardly the style collapsed. There was a hollow inside and some of them had no way of coping with what had happened. It raised fundamental questions about their own stories. Why had their priorities taken so little account of this possibility? Why had all the things that seemed so important and valuable in their lives seem to fade? Does death diminish the meaning we have, does it make what we do less important, would it change our goals if it was part of the life equation? Does this story of ours just come to a sudden halt ... to nothing? If we are to have a full courageous look at life, whether we are believers or non-believers, we should give account of what we think about it. Is it just the final part of an accidental process, or is it the end of the beginning?

As I shall try to show later, the Christian faith above all offers an answer to these questions. But, if we have no belief in the dimension of God, we still have to have some way of looking at the brute fact and decide what it means to us if our life and the lives of those we love ends in nothing. The shrug of the shoulders, and the turning away to get on with today, was no answer for the wife and child of the young man killed in the air crash. Maybe we find the meaning or at least our meaning by trying to improve the lot of the next generation, and we see our purpose as a sort of investment in a future we shall not share. Maybe we decide that that's just the way life is, and there's no alternative to getting on with it and hoping to avoid death for as long as possible. But we still have to face the deaths of those near and dear to us, and if we have no religious belief we have to accept the hard fact that now their lives have no meaning apart from their place in our memories for a moment until we too have no memory. The pleasures and happiness we have invested so much of ourselves in, at death can suddenly disintegrate into nothing. I admire the way that some people come to terms with this fact and I have no desire to undermine such beliefs but however much they despise religious belief, if they do, their beliefs also have to stand up to reality.

I admit I find it difficult to think that I shall come to nothing. The Christian faith has given me so much in providing a framework of hope and promise of wonder and love beyond earthly life. When I doubt this and look into the void, I realize how difficult being reduced to ash and nothing is for our psyche. I find it even more intolerable at this stage in my life to believe that all those people I have known and cherished, who have given me so much, should be nothing now except for some fading photographs and a beloved voice on a tape, and a letter kept in a drawer. As I buried my father's and mother's ashes in a casket in the ground, I was totally convinced it was not the end of them. I thought of them as free, not becoming nothing, but by becoming even more themselves. Their lives now are not just a quintessence of dust like poor Yorick in Hamlet's eye, but alive in a new way.

When expressing the Christian faith about resurrection, it is important to remember that it is faith, not knowledge. We may face the idea of death with hope and trust that the new life after death is true, but we shall not know. We may say we feel we know, we may have assurance or a sense of belonging, but we do not know. This proper agnosticism enlarges sympathy and gives the proper sense of shared human pilgrimage. Birth and death both involve us in a journey through the unknown. To study them together can help us discover the faith that our lives have an eternal purpose and meaning.

Seven

Half-way summary

Before coming to Jesus Christ, here's just a reminder of where I've got to so far. I hope that you are still willing to journey on!

We have looked at the arguments for believing the universe to be a continuing act of creation, rather than a random purposeless accident. The old scientific/religious divide is not necessary, and the new discoveries give us all an opportunity for a new look at the old questions.

New ideas about time and space not only make us think again about eternity but also offer a way of understanding a dimension of God which is free of time and space characteristics.

Science has also recognized that the existence of life on earth is the most amazing reality. The complex relationship between the Earth, the planets, the stars and the wider universe, makes the possibility of a specific act of creation more credible.

Although it is unlikely we shall ever be able to prove the existence of God, it can be a rational response to believe in the probability that God exists. Most of the precious things we believe in and commit ourselves to, cannot be proved either and the non-existence of God also leaves a lot of explaining to do.

If God exists, then we have to face the question 'what sort of God is God?' If God is loving and benevolent, why is there so much suffering and waste in the world? There is a distinction between the suffering and waste in the natural world, and the suffering and waste caused in the world by the conscious sinfulness of the human race. But ultimately God is responsible for his creation.

Nature is in many ways ambivalent. Because they are as they are, rock, fire and water can bring huge benefit or grief. God is responsible for creating this dangerous and risky Earth, but without the element of chance, without life and death, without reliability in the way things are, would life itself be possible, and would human freedom be conceivable?

In some ways the same ambivalence can be discerned in the human race which is poised between bringing benefit and grief. The freedom to exercise self-conscious choice is, however, the fundamental distinction between human beings and the rest of the animal kingdom. This freedom is essential to any proper view of human life. By their God-given conscious will, human beings carry responsibility for much of the damage, waste and suffering on Earth as well as their great achievements for good.

Human conscience has been defined as 'the mind of man making moral judgements'. It is experienced both as positive 'good' conscience in terms of what we think ought to be done, and 'bad' conscience in the sense of self-judgement for what we have done wrong. This mind making moral judgements is not just about specific decisions or actions but is part of the continuous assessment we make of ourselves.

We need to search this inner conversation and try to understand how we function. Conscience does not seem to be limited just to our responsibility for ourselves and for other people, but there is a 'Thou' element within this continuous dialogue. There is one within us to whom we talk and who in some sense talks to us, so that we are not alone. The conscience and 'the moral law within' can be gates into God.

Birth and death are both steps involving the unknown, and both are intrinsic to human life. Yet we seem very reluctant to give much thought to either and the implications they have for our identity and destiny. We live in a culture drenched by images of death in war and media, but we are very unwilling to think through the implication of nothing-ness in death, and we have largely lost our pictures of eternity. Therefore we have no framework for facing the question about our mortality.

Footnote: On the face of it, the discarding of religious belief looks like the bold acceptance of secular reality without the illusions of faith. But the rejection itself can have neurotic elements: such as the absurd concentration on the instant and the contemporary; the refusal to face up to the implications of the loss of faith; the shutdown of the religious imagination; the acceptance of ideas which themselves stand up to testing even less than the religion rejected; and perhaps, above all, the adoption of either a cynical or hopelessly naïve and idealistic view of human beings.

Eight

Discovering Jesus Christ

Now is the time to introduce Jesus into this account of faith. This is the appropriate way, because he stepped into human history at a specific time and place within a development of religious understanding of God. He would not have been seen and interpreted as he was, unless human minds were partly prepared for what his life entailed. He addressed the questions human beings asked and the needs they had, and it is a sobering thought that we still ask many of the same questions and have many of the same needs. The human predicament is subject to such massive changes in practical and technical development but in its essence it remains the same. We are still concerned about what is right and wrong, about what satisfies us, about how to cope with evil and encourage the good. We still face prodigious questions about the tension between the individual and the corporate, the rich and the poor. We are still subject to despair and experience joy. We still face the mystery of birth and death. We are still concerned with the exercise of freedom and the existence of slavery. The list of questions that remain the same is vast and profound and that is one reason why the study of Jesus Christ and, even more important, our relationship with him is still the most exciting, enthralling and essential journey we can make.

I want to ask you to make that journey to discover Jesus Christ afresh. It's important to free ourselves of familiar assumptions which may have grown stale, or not grown at all.

For many of us, Jesus is a well known, if fairly abstract and ancient, image. Maybe from religious education in school or perhaps early Sunday school teaching or from media sources we have some knowledge about Jesus. It is alarming, however, how little is known by so many. But for most, Jesus is a familiar figure left in suspended animation, not experienced in a living relationship. In the world of the moving image and rapid change, Jesus can seem like a static frame, not alive now and not influential right at the heart of our experience. He is above all regarded as a figure in the past, and even that is doubted by some. Like the ancient gods of Greece and Rome, he can be stranded in ancient buildings, statues and pictures, looking rather archaic, lovely, and disconnected from modern life. Maybe this is overstating the case, but I don't think so. Indeed I think many people are beginning to realize how far they have come from Jesus Christ. Pale familiarity with the Palestinian in the long white robe, set to stirring Hollywood music, seen for the umpteenth time after a heavy lunch on Easter Day, is an easy and therefore shallow and unsatisfying way to know the one called the saviour of the world. In my more fearful moments, when my own faith is thin and shaky, I dread that people will regard Jesus in the same way as we regard the ancient gods – just a relic of a bygone age. Without the active love of Christ, both his for us and ours for him, life seems bereft of so much that makes it worthwhile. I already see ideas about human beings which are forming without the ideal, the beauty, the truthfulness, the compassion, the justice which Jesus brought and brings to our world. This leaves a powerful thirst.

It wasn't until I nearly died of dehydration that I fully appreciated how precious and fundamental water is to our lives. I always took it for granted that when I turned on the tap the water would be there, plentiful and wholesome. Suddenly in Africa I discovered what it was like to be without water and discover my life system breaking down. I feel that our society is like that about Jesus Christ: he has been taken for granted for so long that we do not realize what it would be like, what it is like to be without him. I believe that we have to approach him afresh, not just as a real person in history but as a personal presence in our lives. For the modern trained mind this is not easy. We have such a kaleidoscope of complex ideas to cope with, so much technology, such a bewildering pace of life, that it is quite hard to search for simplicity and hard to grasp the idea of God, let alone the belief that God became human. It all smacks of the way people looked at things in the past. Yet I believe it is the clue to our ultimate satisfaction and well-being now.

In the early centuries, many people in the church went down the road of denying that Christ was God from God. They accepted that he was a prophet, the highest prophet. Like the other two religions of 'the Book', Judaism and Islam, they thought the step needed to believe that he was God was a step too far. But the church took that much harder step, and indeed many people died in the name of this belief – namely that Christ was God from God. But although that was one of the most important spiritual struggles of all time, we have to see what a difficult step it is. It will involve us in an exploration of the way in which Jesus Christ relates to the questions and ideas I have expressed in this book about God.

Much has been written about the historical Jesus. I am going to set out simply and briefly my own view, without going too deeply into the arguments. I want to concentrate on the way the Jesus of history relates to our understanding of the creation, to the conscience and the contemporary lives of you and me, which will involve us in what it means for him to be the Christ, the Saviour. Because of the controversies over the Resurrection and other aspects of his life in this generation, I want to state where I stand in terms of the Biblical accounts.

People heard about him first from the witnesses. These were the Apostles, Mary Magdalene, and other followers, as well as the growing number of converts who were close to the events and believed they had come to know that Christ was alive after his death. To begin with, the witness spread by word of mouth. It was a time of oral tradition because of the lack of written material available to most people in society. But there were many vividly remembered events and sayings which were commonly told and recognized by those who had shared Jesus's life. When the number of eyewitnesses began to be reduced by martyrdom or old age, as St Luke said, it became necessary to set out the life of Jesus and the Gospel in a coherent order. The writers of the gospels did not just collect and bind up the tradition, but set about giving some account of the meaning of it all. This they did with their own individual genius as well as with the church's vision and authority. It had become important to preserve the truth about Jesus and it seems clear to me that the early leadership of the church was already exerting authority over what was said about the Lord. Those who had been there, or had later become familiar with the facts of his life and death and resurrection, would have resisted inaccuracy and falsehood. It is my conviction that the witness of the gospels is far more true to the life of Jesus than some theologians and sceptics believe. Of course the gospel writers will have given their interpretation and been influenced by the controversies and experiences of the early church, but none of these compared with the authority of what they knew of the life of Jesus — his sayings, teachings and deeds. The most important question that New Testament critics ask is: 'What must the truth have been and be if people, who believed what they believed, described what they saw and experienced in the way they did?'

Such a process of history is always vulnerable because of the fallibility of witnesses. But these were life-changing events for the people involved and they will have remembered this beloved friend who had given them life more vividly than anything else. Although memory can be misleading, the most important and personal events in the past are as clear as if they happened yesterday. My memory of my father collapsing with a stroke into our bedroom is as vivid as ever in the essentials. The conversation I had with my parents 35 years ago about becoming a priest is as clear as a bell and I remember in vivid detail some of the frightening and happy times I had at school. There is much that has been forgotten, but falling in love with my wife is still fresh in my mind — after about the same period of time as separated the writers of the foundation documents of the New Testament from the Resurrection. The whole process of God becoming a living human being made him vulnerable, from swaddling clothes to shroud, and yet he was in the providence of God. In the same way, I believe that, although the accounts of his life were remembered and written by fallible human beings, they were within the providence of God. To my mind and experience they possess the 'ring of truth' and present a real person who is consistent with the person whom we come to know in faith. This person, Jesus from Nazareth, was unique, not just in the sense that we are all unique human beings but in that his life was marked by a unique relationship with God.

Jesus was an itinerant teacher, who taught by example and through simple stories. His truth and his stories can still have great power and influence in our lives. He was a prophet, speaking for God, especially about the Kingdom of God. This kingdom was found not only through the obedience of his people on Earth, but also in the realm of God above. He was a bridge builder between the dimension of God beyond time and space and the earthly experience. He called people to change and struggle free from their sins and all that diminishes them. He saw that the way to be a whole human being was to have an intimate relationship with God whom he called Father. He warned against the dangers of riches and self-righteousness and he had a profound concern for those who were written off by society. He had the reputation of associating with the failures, and sinners, and found the company of self-righteous hypocrites intolerable.

Jesus taught that religion was primarily a matter of our relationship with God rather than of temple rites and ceremonies, though he was a faithful attender at the synagogue. He was a great moral teacher in the Jewish tradition and there was little that was totally new in his teaching, but he cut away much of the legalistic baggage which cluttered up the basic commandments of God. His preference for the two great commandments was an example of simplification and selection, full of genius, which did not imply any diminution of the law of Moses in its basic principles. Although he had a profoundly sacramental view of life, he was ultimately more concerned about what went on inside people than their possessions and status.

One sign of Jesus' intimacy with God was the miracles.

Jesus was a miracle worker who was much concerned about their effects: when he fed the five thousand, he was distressed to see that they chased after him for bread rather than the truth. He discovered that the miracles did not necessarily bring thankfulness or improvement of soul. He resisted the temptation to use supernatural, miraculous power to win over the people. The miracles were a mixed blessing and Jesus was concerned that the people involved should find not just physical healing but also wholeness of spirit. But there are many miracles in the gospels and the great majority of them are totally free of magicians' tricks, and extravagances and self-aggrandizement, which can be seen in so many other miracle workers of his time. His miracles were consistent with his teaching and example, signs of what life could be like when the physical and the spiritual are properly integrated. To remove them from the gospel witness, and to remove the miraculous from his life, would be to leave a pale image of the man himself.

Our greater difficulty is the doubt that miracles can happen at all. I am convinced that healing events still take place which have no perceived physical explanation, appearing to be the result of prayer and faith. If you believe in the Kingdom of God, there is nothing intrinsically impossible in miracles. We have already discussed the existence of an eternal dimension, which is so different to the universe, which operates by different rules. We have also given thought to the bridge that can be built by God between the two types of existence: the eternal and the temporal realms of the universe, the Kingdom of God and the natural physical kingdom. If we could see the eternal and understand it, we could see that the miraculous was consistent with the overall purpose of God. It would be the height of arrogance and the denial of faith to say that God could not intervene in earthly life. Christ himself is an intervention.

But now, as then, there are false miracle workers about and they do a great deal of damage. Miracles can still carry a serious downside. How do we deal with the fact that a miracle happens in one situation and not in another? Why does one baby survive in a miraculous way when millions starve? How do we tackle the guilt and despair of those for whom the miracle does not happen? Now, as then, a miracle still attracts a lot of undesirable attention. The best faith-healers I have known, like Jesus, try to keep it discreet. They don't ride the power. They don't appeal to the infantile response which develops a sort of addiction to the super-natural. They recognize the dangers and difficulties involved. In praying for healing we are always praying for the love of God, recognizing that any intervention which breaks through our understanding of the natural laws has to be within His overall purpose. Miracles can bring faith and overwhelming joy but they are not uncomplicated.

Part of the complication is the way they fit into a scientific view. Why, when the consistency of nature is so necessary to our knowledge and action, would God change the rules in particular circumstances? The universe itself is sufficient evidence of his power. But miracles, although they were seen as signs of Jesus' power, were primarily examples of his love. We are not sure how love fits in to the law of nature. In a way it seems like an intrusion into the way things work. We sense in Jesus the struggle to demonstrate that God the Father is the God of love. It remains remarkable and therefore, in terms of evidence, important that Jesus expresses such reserve about his miraculous acts of love. The temptation was for him to use them to demonstrate his power. Someone once said that the problem is not that people do not believe anything, but rather that they believe *any thing*. I have tried to set out a way of thinking through faith and, in the case of miracles, thinking is especially needed because people's desire and need for healing is so great. There is so much quackery in our world today, as there was in Jesus' day, and it can lead people seriously astray in the search for God. But our proper desire that we should support, finance and value medical research and care should not exclude initiatives of God within his purpose of love for the world.

By prayer, by faith, by trust in Christ, healing is possible but we have to recognize that we do not understand the overall purpose of love nor why it works a 'miracle' in one instance and a long sustained and painful death in another. We shall not answer many questions in this journey. The pursuit of truth is extremely important but it is limited to our perceptions. There can seem to be a sort of arrogance in saying that because we have scientific knowledge certain things cannot happen.

This is especially true of the best-witnessed events of Jesus' life – the Passion and the Resurrection. It is as if the story was told from the end back to the beginning. Although his followers had experienced his ministry to have been compelling and inspirational, it was because of his last days that the whole story was told. We hear about Jesus in the light of what happened in his agony, his trial, his crucifixion, his Resurrection appearances and the other experiences of the eyewitnesses. He suffered not just in the physical pain and psychological grief but in the spirit, through the burden of humankind which he carried. He believed that he was dying to save us, and part of his suffering was his own doubt and sorrow and his own despairing moments. Here was no anaesthetized, untouchable, immune superman who was somehow playing games with the experience and with his opponents, but a real man who cried out in pain and fear, whose heart was ready to break, who felt the grief of the loss of life and loved ones. He lived through the human tragedy in a representative way and identified with the human predicament. The four gospels are sometimes inconsistent in detail and certainly the events are often described in different ways, but again the overall consistency is remarkable and the writers do not let their own vision run away with them because they had basic facts to deal with under the eye of the church. Yet the apostles are not glorified, indeed in several ways they make a poor showing. Nor do the writers draw back from telling the story in ways that would have given offence to their own assumptions. They tackle brilliantly the almost impossible task of revealing to us someone who was both Son of Man and Son of God.

But death on the cross and the burial in the tomb was not the end of the Gospel, and they had to record the events which followed his death. These were events unlike any others and not therefore easily described in simple earthly terms. What happened next shines as light back over the whole story. There are very few explanations, because they didn't know any. They began to see reasons why the Resurrection happened but, apart from some basic facts and eyewitness accounts, we are left with a mystery. Jesus was seen to be alive after his death. He was seen and experienced but no explanation is given of how God worked this greatest of miracles. It is plainly not a conjuring trick. It is some bridge between the human earthly dimension in time and space and the eternal dimension of God and, not surprisingly, there was confusion all round. I shall be saying more about this experience later but for now I want to affirm that I believe that Jesus did defeat death, that he was seen to be alive and that the tomb was empty, and that these bewildered witnesses have provided what we need: to discover the faith that Christ rose from the dead and is with us as we journey on the road. The authenticity of the life and truth of Jesus lends weight to the belief that such a person was unique, and therefore could open the gate of Heaven in ways we don't totally understand.

A movement followed these events. It was a movement which began without any earthly power, but grew with amazing speed. The people involved were convinced not only that Christ had risen from the dead, but that he was present with them in the Spirit. This movement became a vast organization, with power and vice as well as the beauty of the saints and the holiness of dedicated people. It has always found the capacity to be reborn, and to discover afresh the Resurrection of Jesus, both as an event in the past and as an event in the present. There are dark ages, and there are hellish times for the church, but we are witnesses to the renewal and rebirth of faith in our own day throughout the world, which demonstrate the universality of Christ. It is to this claim which I now turn.

Whether we are a great scientist or a simple peasant, when we face the universe we face impenetrable mystery and holiness. We stand at the edge of an ocean looking into an immensity we can hardly begin to grasp. The more a person prays – though only a tiny speck in this universe both in terms of time and space – the more the soul opens up the sense of a loving creator. We can discover and experience a sense of the divine in and through everything, and this discovery leads to an ever deeper reverence. Carl Sagan, in his introduction to Stephen Hawking's *A Brief History of Time*, sums up its conclusions: 'A universe with no edge in space, no beginning or end in time, and nothing for a creator to do.' Whilst this reflects much that is said in the book, Hawking's final words are these:

> However, if we do discover a complete theory, it should in time be understandable in broad principle by everyone, not just a few scientists. Then we shall all, philosophers, scientists and just ordinary people, be able to take part in the discussion of the question of why it is that we and the universe exist. If we can find the answer to that, it would be the ultimate triumph of human reason — for then we would know the mind of God.

The encounter between scientific exploration and theology is exciting, even if sometimes approached with scepticism, but I feel there is a new openness to the possibility of God. Even the most self-contained universe can be filled with God. The claim that God does not exist certainly ignores or explains away the experience of those who pray and discover the sense of the holy in everything. But at this moment my concern is to see how Christ might be involved in the process whereby everything came to be and continues till now.

We face two specific dangers as we approach Christ in the third millennium. The first is that we shall allow him to slip away from our consciousness, and the second that we shall claim too great a familiarity with him. This book is concerned primarily with the first of these dangers. It is my hope that some who are now allowing the door of their hearts to close silently will open it wide to Christ. But I also find that some of the renewal movement in the church claims and expresses a familiarity with Christ which makes him seem small. The familiarity appears to bypass the mystery. It is so easy to lose some of the sense of the holy we ought to taste as we approach God. Part of this familiarity stems from our inability to have a vision of Christ in creation, which in turn derives from an inadequate idea of creation itself. Yet, as I have tried to suggest, this present generation has so many new thoughts, ideas and scientific advances to use as analogies or parables to explore the universe and God that it should be more possible to see how Jesus of history can relate to this creation story.

I have tried to show how we can think of God the creator as being in his own dimension outside time and space. The New Testament writers use the word translated as 'eternal' to describe this other dimension. The ancient teaching of the church is that Christ is also eternal. That is to say that when we talk about God before the beginning of time and outside space, Christ was already in God. The love of God for his creation and for the human race was, from the beginning, Christ-like. This human face of God became a man. According to this faith, Jesus was not just a Palestinian Jew but also the Christ, the way in which God expressed the profound love and compassion he has for his world and for humanity. It is shown to us through the relationship between a father and a son, a communication is given through what we know and experience as human beings.

Communication itself is one of the most helpful windows into God and Christ. Those of you who are familiar with the Bible, or perhaps even just come to church at Christmas, will realize that this is not some new idea conjured up by me but which comes from both the Old and the New Testaments. But it is an idea whose time has returned. We are in an age of vast communication expansion. As with so much technological advance, this revolution has been achieved by unravelling and harnessing the capacities that already exist in the universe. Communication happens at the macro-level, between galaxies and stars, not just in light and sound but in energy, by attraction and resistance. But it also permeates the micro-levels – cell signalling to cell, genes transporting personal messages. In one sense there is communication in and through everything.

It was an ancient idea that there was some sort of universal principle throughout everything – an all embracing network in reality. It is an idea which features in the Bible. Indeed right at the heart of the creation story, God is portrayed as speaking and creating. God said, 'Let there be light' – and there was light (Genesis 1.3). The seven days of creation are the direct result of God's command. The idea appears again in the way wisdom is described in Proverbs chapter 8. Here God uses 'wisdom' (the feminine noun) almost like a person, in the whole act of creation. 'The Lord possessed me at the beginning of his work, before his deeds of old: I was appointed from eternity, from the beginning, before the world began' (Proverbs 8.22, 23). Wisdom communicates throughout the whole universe and is at God's side in the creation itself. 'Then I was the craftsman at his side. I was filled with delight day after day, rejoicing always in his presence, rejoicing in his whole world and delighting in mankind' (ibid. vv. 30, 31). We catch a glimpse of this communication in praying for people, when we see the effect it has on both the parties involved. We see it in relationships. We see it in the idea of a collective unconscious, we see it constantly in micro- and macro-realities.

But to me the most exciting and mind-opening example comes in the first chapter of St John's gospel, where the image of the Word is used as the agent of God in the making of everything. But this 'Word' is not just the agent through whom the universe is created, it is God Himself. The Word was with God from the beginning before anything existed in time or space. In the dimension of God there was the Word. This Word, or communication, was within everything that came to be. Nothing came into existence without this communication. It was the way that God in eternity related to the universe in time and space. St John then makes one of the greatest leaps of faith in the famous phrase: 'The word became flesh' (John 1.14). St John portrays Jesus as the eternal Christ. He was with God from the beginning, before time and space began. In one sense we can't say before time, because the word 'before' is itself a time category. But what it implies is the timeless reality of the eternal dimension of God from whom the universe derived.

In terms of prayer and spiritual experience, this belief that Christ is eternal is deeply significant. It opens up the door to a relationship with him through the everyday experiences, our thoughts and feelings. It also links our love of God the

Son to our love of the Creator. The failure to make clear this link is one of the causes of the strength of the appeal of the New Age and of oriental religion. Christians need a greater sense of the mystery and holiness of Christ as the communication of God through whom everything has its being. It is especially helpful in the sacramental understanding because the bread and the wine communicate with us the loving presence of God in Christ. It also helps us to see the God in the creation as a Christ-like God. However much in Christian doctrine we speak about three persons in the Godhead, we need to remind ourselves all the time that God is one. In the domes and apses of Byzantine churches, the face of Christ is often shown over-arching the sanctuary with his hand raised in blessing. He is called Christ Pantokrator: that is, Christ the creator of all. There is usually also the Alpha and the Omega, the first and last letters of the Greek alphabet, which symbolize the teaching that Christ is Lord of the universe from beginning to end. He is God from God, the bridge builder, the communication between the universe and eternity. These ideas are a source of that most needed of attitudes in our own day – reverence. It gives definition and character to the 'Thou' which faith discerns, yet does not reduce Christ to just a human life ... even that life.

When we draw near to him, we stand on holy ground. Our yearning and longing for God is somehow fed and our thirst quenched. We are lifted out of our shallow selves, from our wasted time and our self-absorption, into the love of God in Christ. This can open up the deep and profound spaces within us. He brings an intensity of the love for the world around us, so that we sense a new way of feeling and seeing. It must be rather like the way in which a poet or an artist's eyes are open to the truth or the sharp perception of the way things really are. 'Eyes have they and they see not, ears have they and they hear not', is the way Isaiah described those who were unable to perceive the true God, who couldn't grasp the inner reality and beautiful immensity of the creation (Isaiah 43.8).

When we read the gospels, listen to the sacred music, see the art, experience the architecture and sculpture which tell the story of Jesus Christ through two thousand years, we realize how much is concerned with the bridge between the eternal and time. It mostly comes from the inspiration of the New Testament. The veil between eternity and the Earth, in Christ, became thin. Although Jesus lived in history from the time of Herod to Pontius Pilate, the eternal Kingdom of God was often breaking through. The dimension of God, the Kingdom of Heaven, is able to shine through the canvas. Perhaps we can use the analogy of the ozone layer, but with the difference that the 'holes' are good and we glimpse the wonder of the healing Son. At his birth the shepherds saw a great light and heard heavenly music. At his baptism the clouds opened and the sun shone and there was a dove flying around his head and a voice from Heaven. At the transfiguration, with his friends on the mountain, Jesus was seen breaking the limitation of time and space, and talking with Moses and Elijah. At the Crucifixion, darkness descended on Jerusalem but no angel of God came to comfort or rescue him as he suffered and died. But then, supremely at the Resurrection, Jesus was moving between the eternal and world dimensions.

There are those who think this is all poetic licence, just the way in which the gospel writers managed to make their own theological point of view known. But I prefer to see it as their way of describing the transdimensional experience of the living Christ. Again, like the miracles, the divine shining through is not over-elaborate, or full of magic high-jinks, but is more like an intense vision of true being. Everything that is described is consistent with the Jesus in time, and the Gospel he proclaimed.

But if Christ was in and through all that came to be, there remains the problem of suffering and waste caused by the nature of the creation itself. Here again I think the understanding of his involvement from the beginning as the Word of God helps. If the communication of God was present in a personal way in the act and sustaining of creation, it shows that this prodigious continuing event has God at its heart and through its system. This is what people of all ages have believed. 'Teach me my God and King in all things Thee to see.' But whilst it is easy to believe in God in the sunset or the peacock or the Mass in B minor, it is not so easy to see him in the ugly, the loathsome and the dying. Jesus obviously shared the faith in the loving creator who loved the world from the beginning. He saw there was no area of life where this creator was not present in love or judgement. If a sparrow falls to the ground, he taught, the heavenly Father knows it. Even the hairs on our head are numbered. He saw signs and symbols of the love of God all around him and he recognized that there was a sort of givenness about the way the universe worked – the rain falls on the just and the unjust.

The universe is full of apparent waste and void. The Earth is full of suffering and dying. Yet the universe and the Earth are full of the wisdom of God. We think of the Cross as tackling the suffering of the world and so it does, but it communicates the way God had always loved the creation from the beginning and the way he will love it to the end. He gave it all life, with the struggles, the pain and the dying as part of the cost of life. We might say that we would like a different world, where the lion lies down with the lamb, where there is no battle for survival, where the strong do not triumph; but in the world we have we can only alleviate the pain and strive for the good and the beautiful. For our brief span we should live the life we have been given to the full. The blackbird dying in the ditch has to accept innocent powerlessness as an earthly creature, with all the risks that life involves. The Word of God is there. The Word of God is in all things that came to be. The Word of God died as a powerless human on the Cross to save the world.

When a person discovers Jesus Christ, there is this powerful feeling that we have discovered what we have always known from the beginning, that there is God in us. When the heart breaks, he is there, as he was in the beginning and will always be, because his heart was ready to break with grief. He gave up the ghost, and the breath of life left him, out of love for the world.

Our own human experience is where we can see Christ in the most personal and direct way. I understand those who only want to talk about this aspect of his love, because it can be overwhelming. It can seem the only important feature of faith, rather like falling in love totally absorbs us. All that I have written is important to my faith, but now I come to the heart of the matter. Christ experienced humanness. He loved and laughed and cried and struggled and hoped and feared. He not only gave himself for humankind, but he gave himself for *me*. This personal longing for the love of Christ sounds so self-centred, like a spoilt child who wants to have all the attention and love for himself. But it's not like that because, when we realize we are loved by Christ, in a strange way it begins to free us from self-concern. God willing, he shows us outgoing love like his, and motivates us to follow his way. His love asks for service and sacrifice, and so breaks the pattern of absorbed self-interest. Christ demonstrates the love of God from the beginning. His life, death and resurrection do not change God's mind; they are God's mind at work. To me life would be so diminished if we had no Christ, not just because of what he taught and did but because of what he is for the world – yes, and for me.

It is not easy to find Christ if you think you have no need of God. I know this is a big discouragement for people who don't like to admit their need. I remember a time when I used to think like that, but now I realize there has to be an openness to the possibility of God and a recognition of some yearning or longing for the love of God. However, God has demonstrated on many occasions that it is possible, even when we resist him, for us to be changed. The transformation can at first seem almost against our will, but later turns out to be what, beneath the bravado, we most wanted. When we look back there was often an emptiness and unfulfilled longing. If we feel totally self-absorbed, or self-sufficient, it should not surprise us that God has not been able to penetrate our defences – such is the freedom he gives us. If, however, we look for him, search with humility of mind, then the gate is already open.

To need God, as I have said, is no more of an admission of weakness than to need food, drink or love. Although the need can take many different forms, it is there because it's the way we are. I often listen to those who despise and mock faith in God, and I feel pity because it can be obvious that much of their own life is chewed up by their determination to be self-sufficient. I guess they feel sceptical about me because they think I have invented this God because of my own need. I see this as one of the prime reasons why the dialogue between believers and others can be so difficult. It is hard when you have an overwhelmingly beautiful experience of God, not to feel that everyone should feel the same way. I hope anyone who has read this far, or just opened the book at this page, might not be ashamed of their need but see it as a possible door to God. Some of the greatest people I have known have fallen to their knees in prayer on a daily basis – both in their need to tackle their enormous tasks and also on the basis of their need as children of God. There is no shame in that. It is an expression of our proper dependence on the source of life. There are as many doors as there are people, but for many the 'need door' is blocked. This is strange because for many others it's the only door that's open. The danger of the 'need' route is to make a God who is defined by our own personal requirements and specification.

The other personal door to discovering God, which I identified earlier, is conscience. This is not conscience in the narrow sense, but referring to the whole self as moral being. There are so many struggles here. What is right and what is wrong? How can I be the person I know I ought to be? How can I cope with the times, both serious and minor, when I have betrayed and continue to betray what I know to be right? How is it that I am so insensitive to the needs of other people, even those I claim to love? How can I forgive others, and how can I forgive myself? When I look at my own failings, they are heavy enough; but what about those failings writ large in family, community, nation and world? What steps could we have taken to tackle the injustice of the world? How can we face our responsibilities in the midst of society, to bring about change, to do the good we could? What are we to do with guilt? What part does punishment play in the just society and in our own lives? Why do we get so depressed about the person we are? Will we never be able to change? Are we just a product of our past and our social environment, or do we have our own freedom to choose and to impress some creative pattern on our lives? The questions are endless. They are the constant theme of the human journey, and it is at the personal source of identity in the conscience that I want to show how Christ can not only help but is, in a real sense, the answer. This does not just concern us as individuals, but as community in collective attitude and action.

We have almost all experienced love at some time. Some have it at the centre of their lives, whereas for others it is just a memory. It remains the best analogy of the way in which Christ affects, or can affect, our lives. When 1 Corinthians chapter 13 is read well in church, you can hear a pin drop. It's because everyone recognizes in St Paul's great words our deepest aim and longing. It is what we are about. St Paul wrote his masterpiece after reflecting on the love he had received from Jesus. If we have not yet tuned in to the love of Jesus, we can see it reflected in the love we receive in our own relationships. When we are loved and we know it, we travel with a fair wind. We can always return to this love, remind ourselves of it, relish the communion it brings. To be loved gives us a far stronger sense of our own identity, and we grow as we are able to love in return. By enabling us to develop self-respect and concern for others, love changes our values. If we are people trapped in a low opinion of ourselves, to be loved brings a new freedom and the realization that, despite all our worst suspicions, we are lovable. Love is unconditional and it doesn't depend upon attraction, though it is easier if there is attraction between two people. Love does not approve of everything we do – in fact love is vulnerable to our betrayals, our mistrust and denials – yet love is steadfast, because it sees and understands the wrong paths we take, and is there when we come to our senses. But love requires a lot of us, not in a possessive way, but in a way which calls us to be the best we can be. Love often makes sacrifices for us, but doesn't make capital out of it. Love offers us hope and freedom to be and to choose and to grow to maturity. All this and much more describes what it means to believe we are loved by Christ, who was attracted to us all enough to die for us.

Love at work in the conscience is also transforming. We know this from our own experience and see it at work in others. As a priest I have seen people emerge from depression, from self-pity and fear, and shine with the strength of his love in their lives. They begin to blossom. They no longer hide their talents and gifts out of a sense of inadequacy or the dread of being made to appear fools, nor carry a crippling sense of guilt. I have seen people who, in this love, have been able to turn impossible situations, illness and defeat into new opportunity. But sometimes people are unaware that they are loved and never feel the warmth of its blessing. Sometimes love is ignored or rejected, like the love of parents whose children become drug addicts and abuse them, or of a child who is being torn apart by its parents' rows and is trying to bear the pain of a loveless marriage. These are parables of what it must be like for God to see his love rejected and misused. He saw it on the Cross. Like a hen longs to gather her chicks under her wings – that was the way he longed for his children when they were lost. God loves us in every moment, but we can't see it.

We plunge further into darkness, when we rebel against what is best for us. That has such a parental ring, like 'cabbage is good for you', or 'early to bed'. But the painful truth is that parents sometimes do know better than children. God is a loving parent, who knows from the beginning what we can be. When we see what we ought to do, and don't; when we see what we ought not to do, and then do it; then we know from experience that it hurts not only others but also ourselves. Shame and guilt hurt. They can hurt so much we can't bear it. Then we turn it into something else: depression, aggression, resentment, hate, etc. The human story in the Bible begins with this. Adam and Eve rebel and discover alienation, and then Cain turns his jealousy into violence against his brother. His guilt condemns him even from Abel's blood on the stones, and Cain cries out a universal complaint, 'Am I my brother's keeper?' (Genesis 4.9). He turns away from himself and goes into the exile of the land of Nod, East of Eden. His punishment was too hard to bear. We all experience shame, and to meet someone who has only shame left, or whose conscience has died, is to meet someone trapped East of Eden, with a dreadful mark in their eyes of a lost and imprisoned soul. It is a hard and heavy burden to carry unforgiveness and to believe that we can never be forgiven.

Like love, the effects of forgiveness are transforming. It is wonderful to feel hope and self-respect return, to feel free of past wrongs, and laugh again without that undercurrent of despair. It is a great force for good in our world. It is not cheap, though it doesn't cost money. Forgiveness is not soft and flabby. We make such a mistake when we think of it as automatic, with no cost or reparation. Forgiveness comes when we see what we have done and take responsibility for it, when we repent and ask to be forgiven, seek to make amends and, where possible, make reparation. As we know from those times when we have managed to forgive someone who has really hurt us, it's a costly business. We feel boiling resentment and anger. We feel that justice requires the person to make some reparation, or at least to accept the blame. If a person mugs or rapes another, we all want to see that person pay for what they have done. There are not many victims who find it in their heart to forgive. When we meet such forgiveness we are on holy ground. The best most of us can do, in each circumstance, is to walk away and avert our eyes. No – forgiveness is *not* cheap, neither for us nor for God.

The present experiment in bringing together criminals and their victims has a sign of hope in it. It can be a way to repentance and new attitudes. We often don't see the results of what we have done to others and therefore do not realize the harm we have done to ourselves and our conscience. There is no forgiveness without cost. If we confess our sins to a priest or a counsellor or a friend, they will not say, if they're doing their job, 'it doesn't matter'. They may say we're getting it out of proportion, or that we haven't seen half of it, but they would let us down if they had so little love and respect for us that they didn't have the guts to reflect the cost of what we have done. Sin is an expensive business in the moral being of a person.

Jesus provides the answer to this universal and continuing human problem. This huge claim will not appeal to any reader who thinks they have never and will never require serious forgiveness, but for the rest of us Jesus is a challenge and a comfort. He is not an easy answer like a scratch card, or a rabbit produced out of a hat. But many of us can bear witness that his acceptance, his love and forgiveness are the most important experience of our lives. It is likely that a person released from jail knows more about freedom than someone who has never been imprisoned. I am not just talking about the prisons to which we are sent by a court of law, but the prisons we build for ourselves, lock ourselves in and sometimes throw away the key. Jesus does stand at the door and knock. His life was a demonstration of that life-giving hope which came from his offer of redemption, acceptance, judgement and forgiveness. This redemption means being freed from prison or slavery. It may look a vague and abstract word but our addictions, our blindness, and our resentment need a powerful cure. Right at the heart of the story of Jesus' life and teaching, and his giving of himself even to the point of death, was this offer of paying the ultimate price of our wrongdoing. We still have to face up to what we do, but we are opened up to the future freed from the burden of our past.

Almost every page of the New Testament has an encounter, a parable or an act of forgiveness in it. It has the seriousness of the judgement, but the overwhelming message is the longing of God for us to see and find freedom. In prayer Jesus taught, 'Forgive us our sins, as we forgive those who have sinned against us' (Luke 11.3–4). He often told people who were ill not only that their faith had healed them but also that their sins were forgiven. In his parables of the prodigal son, the unforgiving debtor, the lost sheep and many others, he offers the forgiveness of God. Supremely on the Cross, looking at the crowds who had colluded with those in power, he was still forgiving, and to the thief he said, 'Today you will be with me in paradise.' People get so angry because it seems so weak to forgive, but in Christ a profound price is being paid. It cost God the life of his Son. This does not mean that somehow God got someone else to do his dirty work for him. The love of God himself, expressed in terms of a loving relationship, paid the ultimate sacrifice for his creation.

Even when we ourselves forgive we have to make sacrifices. We have to give up our anger and hate, let go of the satisfaction of seeing the other person being punished and getting their just rewards. We have all tasted this bitter pill. When we are the offender, we also have to pay a heavy cost. It is not easy to accept that we have done wrong and bear the shame when we face it. Repentance involves painful change and to receive forgiveness is humbling. But as soon as we tackle the cause of the sin in our soul, we experience the new future, sloughing off our old skin. The church goes on about sin, because it's that which fouls up our world. It hurts both the offender and the victim, and it festers as long as it is not worked out of our system.

It is not just the sin we do as individuals, but the wrong we do corporately. Most of the time, our corporate sin is infinitely worse. This is something that we find it difficult to accept in our country. Some politicians seem to want to place responsibility always on the individual but, whilst individuals contribute to the overall total of corporate sin, our combined action almost takes on a will of its own, expressed in political decisions and collective attitudes. Just think of the indescribable inhumanity of nation to nation. We would never dream of starving children to death as individuals but as nations we are relatively untroubled when we share in causing it. Or on a domestic level, it seems so little and insignificant when we drive our cars, and yet our combined driving is polluting the atmosphere, damaging our future and our children's future. Nations find it difficult to accept their guilt and make reparation unless it is forced on them. In economics, we are glad when our balance of payments improves, without noticing how the improvement in our living standards has impoverished others who are much poorer than ourselves. We sell arms to countries whose people have no food, we allow the vast international debt to keep whole nations at the bare survival level if they're lucky. Or perhaps we own shares in a company which is profiteering at the expense of the poor. There are also all the ways in which we have maltreated the other members of the animal kingdom, through our own corporate attitude, and the ways in which we have polluted the beautiful creation we have been given. One of the ways in which our shared attitudes cause suffering on a big scale is by tolerating and indeed sometimes encouraging prejudice in legislation, policing and imprisonment and so encouraging racial hatred and bigotry to grow and fester. Often we shelter behind the policies and actions of our community as a whole in order to do things which we would hate to do ourselves, or at least hate to be seen to be doing ourselves.

The power and weight of corporate, collective wrong-doing is vast. It continues to breed from generation to generation and it can be totally overwhelming. It can be so attractive to think, 'I'll just stay in my own little safe corner ... as long as no-one interferes with me ... that's all right by me ... Eat drink and be merry, for tomorrow we die.' This individual, privatized view of society and of politics is plain wickedness. It's simply not good enough to opt out and concentrate on our own well-being alone. It is not only wrong; it doesn't work. Acid rain doesn't recognize national, let alone personal, boundaries. The holes in the ozone layer won't be healed just over the spot where we live. Poverty produces violence which hurts all of us. Racism brings conflict in society as well as polluting our souls.

One of the most common hiding places is the cellar of the cynics. It is so easy to avoid commitment behind the clever tearing apart of the efforts that others make. Nothing seems to reassure us so well as the despair about ever doing anything, or the enjoyment of proving that the people who fight for the right and the good have all got skeletons in their own cupboard. There was a recent television programme which tore to shreds the work and personality of Mother Teresa. Of course there are things to criticize in such an international work as hers, but it's such an easy way out to show that no one is pure, no one is as good as they seem, no aid organization deals properly with the money they receive, no politician really wants to make a better world, just so we can all hide without the discomfort of the corporate conscience. Cynics produce clever arguments for doing nothing.

To me it is important that Christ did not just die for individuals. The story of God's care for the world has been much more of a care for humankind. God's care for Israel had the ultimate purpose of the salvation of all peoples. Certainly Christ is not merely an individual saviour, he died to save the world. He died that people would be changed and, by their obedience to God, take steps to tackle the problems of the world. Therefore we can't hide away from the struggle, but rather are called to make our own contribution. I love the Zambian hymn which says 'Don't say you have nothing to give, just give'. Perhaps there should be a second verse: 'Don't say there's nothing you can do, just do.' But, as all those know who have tried to change the world or just a little part of it, the burden and weight of even our little bit is heavy. The sustaining love and strength of Christ is so great a force for good in the face of this struggle. He is right at the heart of it all. He is the sign of God which says that ultimately good will triumph. He is the greatest antidote to despair. He gives his spirit of hope and encouragement to those who soldier on. He enables the smile, the love and the bloody-minded determination not to be defeated. He also bears the past and is a great instrument of forgiveness at a corporate and collective level.

Perhaps above all the love of God, expressed in Christ in society and international relations, is the call to justice. Justice is the way that love takes collective form in our world. Of course the Christian community has many times in history betrayed its Lord, but the Kingdom that Christ preached is a kingdom where justice rules at an individual level and at a collective, national and international level. The world as we know it has the potential for massive suffering and waste, and the human race within it is capable of the most hideous of crimes, both individually and corporately. But there is also the wonderful possibility of individuals and societies and nations and the international community working for the common good. We see much that is disheartening and life-threatening but there are also signs of hope – solid achievements because people had the guts and the tenacity to strive and, by their co-operation and commitment, bring improvement or ease the suffering. It is the cost of freedom that any steps towards justice and peace, which are the goals of the Kingdom of God, require courage, vision, love and commitment. These are the goals of the God who created the universe; who loved it so much, gave it its freedom to be, did not abandon it to its failure but went on loving it. Jesus Christ gives us the perfect image of how much God cares for the world, and at the same time calls us to be disciples who seek the Kingdom of God on Earth as in Heaven.

The scar of evil, derived from God's offer of freedom, needed some vast source of hope and healing from God. In the love of the Son, God has shared in the struggle, and shown that he shares now with all those who suffer. They are not cut off from God however much their hearts may be breaking with grief. He is especially close to them. He calls us to share in the task of saving the world by recognizing the responsibility we all have. He calls us to strengthen and support all those movements of the human spirit which point to the Kingdom, which take steps in the mutual and shared task set before us. It is this task which gives us our purpose and our destiny. If we look realistically at the false hopes, the false gods which tempt us to think they provide the solution to our problems, the depth and wonder of Christ towers over such alternatives. Yet somehow now we are letting the light of Christ fade against the dazzling, often trashy lights of the contemporary amusement arcade. How deeply we need his hope, his faith and love, to challenge so many assumptions of society and, sadly, sometimes the church.

Nine

Loving

On centre stage in Christian ethics therefore is the imperative to love. This is not just a matter of 'feeling' but also a commandment – indeed, Jesus summarized the whole law with these words: 'You shall love the Lord your God with all your heart, with all your soul, with all your mind, and with all your strength and your neighbour as yourself.' Or, as St John wrote,

> Those who do not love their brothers and sisters whom they have seen – how can they claim to love God who is unseen? (1 John 4.20)

As we have seen, alongside 'love' must go 'justice' because justice is love expressed in communities and nations. In human relationships, whether between individuals or collectively, love and justice are the benchmark set by Jesus. This love and justice is to be based on the love we receive from God rather than something which relies solely on our own efforts. It is this loving which is the way that Jesus offers. It answers our deepest needs and clearly sets out what is involved in being a Christian disciple and a Christian community.

People often say, 'Ah, but do they practise what they preach?' It is not difficult to list a catalogue of shame through two thousand years where, in the name of Christ, people and powers have denied him, betraying him with a loving kiss. We who try to live the Christian faith ask ourselves the same question. How can we believe in Jesus Christ and at the same time fall so far short of his calling to love God and love our neighbour? We answer the question by carrying on the struggle to be faithful and good and recognizing not only our own failures but also those of the church. Nowhere is this tension more obvious than in the way we treat other people, whether individuals or communities or nations. The church is a tale of two cities comprising the best and the worst of human behaviour. Alongside the wonder of holiness and goodness, of truth and beauty, of love for the poor, of heroic battles for education and justice, of pastoral love and warmth of fellowship, there has been racism, religious wars, persecutions, hypocrisy and repression. But the church and the Christians are always under the judgement of Jesus Christ as well as encouraged by his forgiveness and love. He has set us a profound example, a way through the human struggle. But it is a very high standard of behaviour, as anyone who tries to 'love their enemies' soon discovers. I would argue that we have a need of an ideal: not to falsify our own identity but to give us a vision of what we might be.

'Love' is a word so often misused. It is a blessing that the Christian version is defined in Jesus himself. From him we learn this love involves self-sacrifice, calls for the giving of ourselves to others, requires a breaking down of the barriers of race, class, religion and gender that divide human beings. Jesus also radically accused the self-righteous and highlighted the goodness in the marginalized and the poor.

He challenges our greed, our lust, our envy, our selfishness, our anger and our pride, showing that the roots of these lie deep within ourselves and need spiritual treatment. So he calls us to 'seek first the Kingdom of God' where God's will is done.

This radical calling is to the human race corporately and collectively as well as to individuals. In the 1980s and 1990s there have been so many attempts by politicians and even some Christians to drive the Christian faith into the private sphere. Salvation is not only a matter for individuals but also for society. Faith is not just a matter of personal belief but involves the saving of the world. Individual piety matters but it has to go with a commitment to tackling injustice, ecology, unemployment, racial prejudice and discrimination.

As Desmond Tutu said of those who condemned his

statements about political issues: 'I wonder which Bible they're reading?' Every Christian shares responsibility within their own sphere of influence for the world in which we live. We can't tackle everything, and most of us do not have access to much power, but we are called to fulfil the potential in us. We all have to play our part in the healing and building of a better world. It may be in political activity or in practical care, or even attempting to influence our place of work towards the goal of greater justice. I think it's harder to stand up in the boardroom of an international company and work for justice than it is for a Bishop to stand up in the pulpit and speak about it.

This does not mean that a life of self-giving love is inevitably swamped by the suffering and wickedness of the world. It's one of the beautiful facts that, though personal commitment to goodness and justice in the world can require tough personal decisions and may require some ultimate self-sacrifice, in the normal run of life it also brings human comradeship, laughter and that deep sense of identity which derives from sharing in the doing of the right. It enables us to discover that profound satisfaction and contentment exists where people are people, not divided and defined by class, gender, colour or even religion. To co-operate with the love and justice of God is to discover the Holy Grail, even if it brings its own burdens of frustration, grief and sacrifice.

Sometimes I fear that religion will become privatized into a merely individual matter. The faith of the church involves a great company of disciples who together make up the Body of Christ, committed to preparing the way for the Kingdom of God on Earth as in Heaven. On the other hand, religion can become so intensely 'collective' that the individual prophet, the lone voice, the eccentric, the dissenter becomes crushed by the corporate judgement. In our society, however, we need to rediscover and act upon the calling to belong to each other, to play our part in a great company, to share responsibility and not retreat into a private holiday brochure to hide from the great issues facing our society and our world. Christians must get involved in their own situation, using their own gifts. It's like in the marathon:

some run like athletes, some hobble to heroism, but all who reach the line are clothed in shining cloaks and have the wonderful sense of achievement not just as individuals but together.

We also have a personal life to live both as individuals and in relationships. Jesus calls us to love our neighbours as ourselves and makes it clear that following this way depends upon our loving God with our whole self in response to his love for us. We know from experience that love requires us to choose how we behave. Quite often we choose the wrong path because we don't see what we're doing to ourselves and others, and sometimes because we deliberately do what we know to be wrong. St Paul expresses the dilemma with frightening accuracy. 'I do not understand what I do. For what I want to do I do not do, but what I hate I do' (Romans 7.15).

Jesus told a parable about a cornfield. An enemy sowed some weeds in the field. 'Let them grow together till the harvest', was Jesus' advice. Otherwise the corn may be damaged. The wheat and the weeds in the field of our spirit grow together. St Paul says it's quite clear which are the weeds and which is the wheat – which is the harvest of our worst nature and which grows from the spirit of God. If we look at his two lists they are still very down-to-earth. 'The harvest of the spirit is love, joy, peace, patience, kindness, goodness, fidelity, gentleness and self-control. There is no law against these!' Whereas the harvest of our unspiritual nature is a longer list: 'fornication, indecency and debauchery, idolatry and sorcery, quarrels, a contentious temper, envy, fits of rage, selfish ambitions, dissensions, party intrigues and jealousies, drinking bouts, orgies and the like' (Galatians 5.19–23). It sounds highly contemporary to our ears except perhaps idolatry and sorcery. But in a way idolatry lurks at the heart of many of the sins in our day when we worship money or power or sex. There's also plenty of religion on offer which is sorcery, or little short of it, such as black magic, the occult and ouija-boards.

It is clear that this contrast between the spirit of love and unspiritual nature, has a profound and far-reaching effect on our human relationships. This is the duty side of our human relationship – our duty to respond to the love of God for us, by loving others. The parent has a duty to love its child, the husband has a duty to love his wife, and the wife a duty to love her husband; we all have a duty to love our neighbours as ourselves. The duty to love is not like the way 'duty' is often portrayed – as a straitjacket or prison sentence – but is a way to fulfilment, a way to live for others which brings the harvest of inner peace, even with the struggles entailed.

But human relationships are not just about duty and fidelity; they are also about our desire and need. I have spoken about the need for intimacy with God. We also long to find relationships which engage our innermost selves: where in friendship or love we discover harmony, where we are no longer fundamentally alone. Bertrand Russell, the atheist philosopher, said that 'all human relationships are at root the vain search for God'. In all my ministry I have observed this deeper need for intimacy and seen how being starved of intimacy is as lethal as physical starving. I think of individuals living in a high-rise block of flats in which no one talks in the lift and where the barricaded doors exclude neighbours as well as burglars. I know so many people where the relationships they had longed for in their family or marriage or friends have turned out to be the vehicle of abuse, manipulation and hate. It remains one of the tragedies of this world when a teenager's whole moral sense has been eliminated by the destruction of intimacy from infancy onwards. It is a sort of living death to be without intimacy of any kind. By intimacy I am not talking about sex, but rather the communion of one spirit with the spirit of another – an earthly parable of the union we can have with God.

Sex, however, is obviously important in our longing for intimacy. One of the reasons why so much sex is disappointing and shameful is that it lacks the intimacy of relationship in the first place: such sex therefore does not intensify intimacy but gives a stronger sense of alienation and loneliness.

There have been few greater changes in attitude in the last twenty years than in our understanding and practice of sexual behaviour. The younger generation seem to have much that is good and strong to offer in their loyalty to friends, their mutual support and enjoyment. Their lack of inhibition, the acceptance of a person's sexual orientation, the relative freedom from unwanted pregnancy, the weakening of taboos can make my generation feel we missed out. Yet at the same time this greater freedom can look more problematical than the system of courtship, marriage and fidelity. Obviously both 'systems' have their strengths and their weakness. So great is the confusion that the Church of England has attempted to assess cohabitation as a possible way through the dilemmas we face because it is the way chosen by a vast number of the present generation. Before we come to that question, however, it is necessary to give the Christian context – the tradition in which the Christian stands.

The implication of the Adam and Eve story is that when they recognized their intimacy they became one flesh and started a new human unit: the family. The development of the tradition set this unity in the context of marriage, whereby two people made a public commitment to each other within the context of their own families and community and their commitment was expressed in vows to God. Divorce was not the intention of God, but rather it had to be allowed because of the disobedience of people to God's commandment, to get them out of the mess they had made by their hardheartedness. Jesus recognizes divorce but still sees it as a serious falling away from what God wants us to do. Marriage does not just depend on the two people involved but on the grafting together of their families, the public witness and support of friends and their community. The marriage was also set within the enabling love and praise of God. God had made a faithful covenant with his people and in the same way husband and wife made a faithful covenant with each other. As Jesus said, divorce was only allowed by Moses because of the hardness of people's hearts.

Thankfully, the Christian view endorsed the positive Jewish view of sexuality. Sex itself was not seen as a device of the devil. It was not regarded as imprisoning the soul or a dark shadow on human goodness. Rather, it is a basic instinct implanted by God which was essential to the flourishing and continuance of the human race. The claim of faith is that God is intimately involved in the whole creation. The Psalmist says to God, 'You it was who fashioned my inward parts: you knit me together in my mother's womb. You know me through and through; my body was no mystery to you when I was formed in secret' (Psalm 139.13–15). Our sexuality was integral to that creation and therefore it is God-given. The difficulty comes with knowing how to express it in the right relationship. Because it is so intimate to our souls, our selves, our bodies, it has special significance. In one sense it affects everything we are, physically and spiritually. It especially affects our relationships. It is a potent source of misuse and abuse of ourselves and others. It is this misuse and abuse which lies at the root of sexual sin. For example, the sin of adultery is the betrayal of a wife or a husband and of children and parents and friends – that is the deception, the damage, the hurt, which the act of adultery does to those who commit it and all those affected by it. Adultery is wrong because of the damage it does to human relationships, not because it involves sex. Promiscuity is wrong because it cheapens and distorts this most intimate of experiences.

Sexuality is good in itself and as part of God's creative plan for human beings but, like our other basic instincts, it has to be used in the service of the good and the loving and not for the denial, betrayal, misuse, and abuse of ourselves or of others. It is a relationship born out of physical and personal attraction and, in the Christian tradition, is based in the love of God. It is a gift based on true intimacy expressed within a faithful covenant relationship where each can rely on the commitment of the other.

The history of marriage, however, reveals that it has often been more a matter of property and finances than this God-given lifelong covenant between two people. It is significant that St Paul's teaching on marriage does not include any mention of property but is an application of his key ethical saying: 'Be subject to one another out of reverence for Christ' (Ephesians 5.21). Although, again, we have questions about the way he applies the principle because of the distinction made between male and female authority: 'Wives be subject to your husbands as though to the Lord.' The complementary response is: 'Husbands love your wives, as Christ loved the church and gave Himself up for it.' Even more dramatically St Paul says, 'Men ought to love their wives, as they love their own bodies.' On the basis of this principle, St Paul moved marriage forward light-years, but still held to the idea that authority is masculine: 'Women must be subject to their husbands in everything.' In recent years many Christians have seen that the principle should lead to both husband and wife being subject to each other, expressing a far more fundamental partnership of equals. Although there are many who would like ethics to stand still where the Bible stands in every particular, it is neither possible nor desirable. Under the guidance of the Holy Spirit, in profound and reverent study of the scriptures, and in prayer, we have to decide where God is leading us now, and in the future, on the basis of the fundamental principles he has given us.

Marriage therefore remains the way the Christian faith teaches us to order man/woman relationships. It is a lifelong commitment: for better for worse, for richer for poorer, in sickness and in health. It is seen as the proper context for sexual relationships, for the family and for the 'mutual society, help and comfort' of the two people who make the commitment. But many people now choose to cohabit (by which I mean not just those living together but also those sleeping together yet still living mostly apart). It must be made clear that here I am not talking about adultery. Adultery implies betrayal and disloyalty to an existing marriage which is clearly sinful; not just according to the Ten Commandments but to every Christian principle. By cohabitation I am talking about people living in a committed relationship either in the same home or not, who express their intimacy by sexual intercourse. It is sometimes very far from marriage but at other times expresses a level of commitment that contains much that would be contained in a commitment to marriage. We need to be more discerning and aware of what can be involved in the decision to live together before marriage, and respect the fact that the decision has often been made in good conscience and mutual responsibility.

The last two generations have come to articulate the fact that commitment can be achieved outside marriage, and can fail to be achieved within it. They also see the contract of marriage as bringing inequality between man and woman, and trapping partners in the social expectations involved. Many young people have known and experienced horrendous broken marriages and have grown up with an image of marriage which seems more like a prison than abundant life. With both women and men pursuing careers and being bound by economic and geographical necessities, and the reluctance of either to give up their career for the other, they decide that they will cohabit. They may well have in mind that in the future they will get married in order to take their relationship into a lifelong commitment. They may especially do this to give their children the stable family which should help them mature in a sense of belonging and wellbeing. Many parents in turn see the strength of these arguments and have their own anxieties about the divorces and separations which have resulted from early marriages when the two people involved are still immature and hardly even know who they are themselves. In this debate the pain of divorce and inappropriate marriages has to be weighed against the weaknesses of cohabitation. For instance, many people plunge into cohabitation only to discover later that they find each other to have changed completely or become totally impossible as partners for life and consequently find the split painful, whether or not it involves divorce.

But cohabitation can aggravate some of the problems associated with marriage. For instance, whilst the partners retain their individual independence and freedom, they can also lack the wider support system of family and friends. So often the family will have got to know and love the partner who then disappears from the scene without further contact. There are also still legal disadvantages for partners in cohabitation compared with marriage, as well as the shadows and stains left for their next relationships to cope with after they decide to part.

There is also the fear that if the first cohabiting relationship broke up then the second will also. The intimacy of the relationship, including the love and commitment, may well not be experienced for the first time and therefore may convey a sense of impermanence to subsequent relationships. Cohabitation involving children carries a whole range of insecurities and may involve the bringing together of children from earlier relationships. Sometimes individuals say they've had no difficulty with these complex sets of relationships, with a selection of parents and grandparents, but it's difficult to imagine how they can replace the special relationship of more sustained and publicly expressed commitment and support. Research gives increasing evidence that divorce does damage to children and, of course, broken cohabitation can cause the same damage.

Another weakness of cohabitation is the lack of social support, which can result in a lower threshold of pain in facing up to the difficulties in the relationship. Marriage is 'for better for worse, for richer for poorer ... till death us do part'. Although this can look like a narrowing-down of human experience it is also an opening-up and a strengthening of the journey. A permanent marriage sees the years between sixty and seventy as important as between twenty and thirty. The human relationship and the intimacy go on growing and are reinforced by the shared history of the relationships themselves. By definition you can't keep track of whole wider families when the partners have several times switched track. All that long-term nourishing and sense of permanence (which of course also has to be worked at, for it is not automatic) gives a context for people to develop their own lives and their individuality. Sadly many people seem to approach marriage too as if it was impermanent and there are corresponding weaknesses in sterile and dreary marriages which so easily lead to fracture.

There are, therefore, forms of cohabitation which are close to marriage but still carry disadvantages. Marriage itself needs a great deal of preparation and support if it is not going to show many of the same weaknesses which are clearly part of cohabitation. For the Christian it is clear that the sexual relationship is seen as 'hallowed and directed aright' within marriage itself, where it grows on the basis of the love and reverence for God which goes on deepening and developing the love for each other. Forgiveness is central to the Christian life and is so essential in marriage as is the practice of praying daily for each other. This is why marriage in church and the faith involved in it is not an optional extra, but the heart of the matter.

One of the strengths of cohabitation is the fact that couples constantly have to renegotiate their contract with each other whereas with marriage it is only too easy to take each other for granted and allow injustice and non-communication to become a way of life. Periodic renegotiation of the marriage relationship is also necessary if people are going to go on growing as individuals within the partnership.

I cannot see a solution to this question at the present time but I believe the church should show compassion, understanding and love (as indeed Christ would have) for those who are doing their best in their circumstances to build their relationship on an honest, loving, sustained faithful basis. At the same time the church has to take greater care over preparation for marriage and to stand firmly for what we believe is the best way.

But, as is often pointed out, not everyone is cohabiting or married and there's a whole company of single people. They contribute hugely to our society and our world. They are often treated as though they don't exist. For those who like to be alone, there is an exciting world to explore and the possibility of a wide variety of human relationships. It's one of the absurd and damaging attitudes in contemporary society that self-realization depends essentially on sexual fulfilment. This tends to magnify the absence of sexual relationships into a personal tragedy or disability and can cast a shadow over the opportunities for intimacy and for self-giving love which do not depend on sexual intimacy. Single people can have a sort of freedom which allows them time and space not only to pursue their interests and beliefs in a committed way but also, in a hectic world, to have the chance of making and sustaining a great variety of friendships which are needed in society and indeed in families today.

There can also be intense pain and loneliness in enforced singleness. The absence of sexual intimacy can loom very large in the life of a person who longs for it, as indeed can the longing for friendship and love of any sort in many people's lives. It is one of the beautiful truths about the church that it often provides a company and a family much bigger and more varied than the individual can find elsewhere. At its heart, it has intimacy with the loving God and from that source of identity and self-acceptance, and the turning away from obsession with our own personal needs, fulfilment can be found. Jesus said that his disciples would find mothers, fathers, brothers, sisters and children and I know that is often true. The life of faith in the company of faith need never be an empty house. A church worthy of the name provides opportunities of sharing in a community, with love at its heart.

In the search for sexual intimacy, which is a big part of growing up, a minority of people discover that sexually they are orientated to people of their own sex and have little or no physical attraction to or sexual desire for the opposite sex. There has in this century been considerable progress in understanding and accepting this fact. In spite of this progress there still remains prejudice against and even persecution of homosexuals, which means that this personal discovery by individuals can be frightening, and thus suppressed, by convention, personal shame and religion, or a powerful mixture of all three.

It is not my task to write a book about homosexuality but rather to think through the Christian faith as the church struggles to come to terms with the changes in understanding which are taking place. As we have seen on other issues, belief in biblical revelation has great strengths but also weaknesses. The strengths are the giving of vision of God especially through history, imagination and experience and the offering of ethical moral wisdom tested and tried through millennia with the illumination that God's light provides. Christ offers the Way, the Truth and the Life. But life did not stop developing when the Bible was completed and bound together in the third century AD. Our understanding of the world and of human relationships – whilst bearing stunning similarities to life then – is also vastly changed by knowledge and experience. Indeed, one of the promises of Christ was that he would send us the Spirit to guide us into all truth.

Christ himself battled with a range of taboos and traditions and reached through those barriers to the individuals in need. He transformed the beliefs about illness (touching lepers, accepting sinners, embracing outcasts), scandalously breaking through religious and racial taboos. It remains shocking to me that people can call themselves his disciples and do not recognize the radical nature of his response to human beings. Time after time he broke through the tight restrictions of the legalistic religion to embrace the person trapped by social condemnation. He was not saying, 'Anything goes' – far from it – rather he called people to a higher righteousness involving greater purity of heart and deeper service of God and of other people. He called people to abundant life, an abundance to be found in self-giving love, in reverence for God, in living the vision of his Kingdom. He recognized people's true identities despite the stereotypes and indeed often revealed the masks worn by the self-righteous who claimed the authority of God. 'Inside they are ravening wolves.'

The Christians who find their identity homosexually orientated, either by intimate life experiences or by genetic character, are faced with a problem. Many abandon God and the church as a result. The treatment such people have received from the church through the centuries makes this an understandable reaction. But in the end we can no more turn away from God than we can turn away from our own identity. There are certain given genetic characteristics in that 'knitting together' in our mother's womb which go to make up the totally unique person. That nature is God-given and loved for what it can become when based on love itself.

The unique nature of an individual will usually be a mixture of what are seen as male and female characteristics. Much damage can be done by repressing our God-given human potential. Most people (if they allow the thoughts and feelings into their minds and do not censor them) will know whether they are largely homosexual or bisexual or heterosexual. It is a true cliché that people in their youth often go through periods of homosexual attraction and then go on to be predominantly heterosexual, but there are also many who know before maturity that they are bisexual or homosexual.

It seems outrageous that we still have to go on saying there is no shame in this human way of being, no reduction of God's love; no cause to feel inadequate or less of a person or handicapped, though it is still a hard life in many ways. Rather, there is in the self a person loved and accepted by God. Therefore he/she should be loved and accepted by the church.

As with heterosexual people, the issue is not one of the person's nature, but rather the person's behaviour. We are all social beings and we all have to tackle our sexuality in human relationships.

The major change since Biblical times is the recognition that homosexuals are not perverted heterosexuals. Heterosexuals, in certain circumstances, use people of their own sex to 'satisfy' their sexual needs, and it is this behaviour which perverts their nature. In St Paul's day this was a familiar part of Hellenistic society. He stood firmly against this perverted feature of the culture which surrounded him. But I doubt whether he or any one else thought that people were homosexual by nature or in their very selves. His strictures against perversion, to my view, still remain true because the domination and misuse of another person of the same sex as a substitute for the other sex is behaviour unacceptable for a Christian.

St Paul's understanding of homosexuality is not the same as today's. It is recognized by most people that homosexuals are who they are and are faced like everyone with the need for human relationships and a desire for intimacy. I return to St Paul's basic premise: 'Be subject to one another out of reverence for Christ.' It is that essential quality of life which should guide the Christian relationship. The description of the harvest of the spirit and the harvest of the lower nature still rings true. For a gay relationship the same Christian ideals apply, the same care, mutual respect and fidelity. The gay 'scene' has been stained, as has the heterosexual, by idolatry and addiction to sex, by physical sexual expression not based in loving relationship, not preserved for that special intimacy which sexual partnership requires. Although I do not believe in gay marriages, because marriage was given to include the procreation of children and specifically created for a heterosexual relationship, I am in favour of strengthening the social support for gay people to have sustained, faithful and loving relationships by legal agreement and by the prayerful support of the church. The harvest of 'indecency', referred to in Galatians, is the harvest of bad abusive relationships. It does not describe loving faithful partnerships between people choosing in conscience to be who at best they can be in the love of Christ.

I am not claiming to know the way forward for Christians. We still have so much to learn about this issue. The church's painful debates may be an opportunity to learn, if they are carried out in prayer and thoughtfulness and based upon a genuine attempt to listen to those who live the question. As for the homosexual people who have turned away from God or church or both, they have their own conscience to be true to. I hope and pray they will see beyond the taboos and misunderstandings to the love of God for them so that they may come to say with conviction, 'By the grace of God I am what I am.' At this time when people can be so judgemental, it's important to remember Jesus' warning to beware of judging people: 'Let him that is without sin cast the first stone' (John 8.7).

Thinking through faith can be a hard business. It requires an openness of mind and spirit and a deep and passionate love for Jesus Christ. He carries so much of our struggle and our grief and bears the sin of the world, and I believe he provides the clue to that most important facet of all our lives: our human relationships and what it means to love our neighbours as ourselves.

Ten

The discovery of God

When I first fell in love, it was as though everything appeared in a different light. Thoughts and feelings were so intense, and I seemed to see so much that I had not seen before. There was a sense of love in the air itself, and I felt as though I had not only discovered my beloved but, by some miracle, I had discovered myself. That experience was very like the encounter with God. It's no accident because God *is* love. That is not to say that falling in love is a replica of the love that God is, but it comes from the same source. The falling in love can become more like the divine love, as it grows in self-giving. Just as love goes on growing and deepening if you stick at it, becoming a source of strength and struggle, enabling you to face more and more reality about yourselves and the world around you, so also sometimes it threatens to slip away and is stained by fear and sin. So it is with loving God. To love and be loved humanly gives an overwhelming sense of purpose in our life and wakes up our hopes and plans for the future and, after a period of total absorption with each other, it begins to flow outwards in children, in family and friends, in community and care about society and respect for others. The discovery of God is very like the unity we can discover with each other. 'Ah, here is bone of my bone and flesh of my flesh' is a parable of the intimate unity we can discover in God. The friendship which grows with love, the desire to be in each other's company, the delight in each other's beloved characteristics are also part of the discovery of God. For some people it seems to happen in a moment but then is worked out in a lifetime, whereas for others it grows slowly.

Why God?

Love between two people is rarely a lifetime of uninterrupted bliss. We all know what it feels like to ache with anxiety about each other, to feel so separate and alone lying in bed together, even to feel that the other person is an enemy who has trapped us and taken away our freedom to live other lives; and so it is with God. We can discover as time goes on that the love can grow deeper as we give ourselves in loving service to each other; and discover that self-giving love is the way, and that self-giving love is the way of God, too.

Maybe you have never fallen in love or have had bad and hurtful experiences in the risk of allowing yourself to love, but this is where the love of God differs from our love, because God's very nature is to love eternally, and his love does not depend upon whether we are beautiful or good or successful, or rich or important or popular. His love is available to all who search for it.

As in friendship we go on learning more about each other, so it is with God. Even in relationships with our friends we only scratch the surface of their personality. So much is hidden in the immensity of ourselves – our millions of thoughts and feelings, the stored memories, the traumas and the fun – yet we can still reach out to know and to love. The discovery of God is reaching out to know an infinite being so that, however much we know, we are still only on the edge of who God finally is. But we can know enough. The little we know is greater than anything else we can know. We can explore him – as we might explore an ocean, or a continent, or space and time – by prayer and by action, by giving ourselves to loving in his world. It doesn't matter whether we come to know him first through his creation, or through Jesus Christ, or through the love and faith of others. The love and faith of others has in my life included friends of other creeds. God can be discovered in the wonder of the stars, the intricacy of a butterfly, the bluebells in the wood, the quiet singing of the whales in the great oceans, or a Formula 1 engine: however and wherever you explore, God is always there ahead of you. I found him under a starry sky, on Christmas night sitting on a tombstone in the frost as the people in church celebrated midnight mass. The initial discovery can come at any time, in any place, and then there is the lifetime of further exploring.

The belief that there is God, if we take it seriously, has a far-reaching effect on us. It brings to our life a reference point, a 'Thou', a source of love and a call to become what we can be. It is in some ways a release from egocentricity. We are no longer satisfied with being self-centred, which is such a barren and rough road, and are given the freedom to love and serve God and discover other people and our world in a new way. The new way takes with it all the progress we have made till then in loving others. In the end it is not just what we say but what we are which defines our relationship with God; though what we say in witness to God is an essential task for a disciple of Jesus Christ.

When you see the universe as filled with God, it begins to increase reverence for life. Some people have this reverence without belief in God, and their reverence for the natural world is part of the redeeming process. When I meet the will of God being done without the confession of faith, I still rejoice and want to join my poor efforts to theirs. There are few more important issues than ecology and what faith in a loving creator calls our 'stewardship' of the world God has given us. Maybe the idea of caring for the world as part of a totally accidental process, which may or may not freeze or overheat to extinction, seems to be enough for some. But to believe that the whole world is the much-loved creation of God, and to recognize that this brings responsibility to the human race and that in reverence for life we are in harmony with what God intends, gives the experience a sense of ultimate purpose and fills it with the beauty of holiness. As I have already argued, ecology is not some prissy flight from the reality of the natural world, but the maximum co-operation with the creator in the world he has given us. As I write this, during an unfamiliar drought, the first rain for three months is falling. The leaves on the tree in the garden are turning to russet and gold, and the greenfinch is already feasting on the red ripe berries, and the cat is watching the greenfinch and wondering whether *he* is ripe for plucking! The amazing provision and the abundance on Earth and the deeply integrated systems which provide food and drink in the whole, give a sense of wonder for God. They also increase the sense of shame and horror that there are millions of homeless and hungry refugees in this fecund world. The discovery of God brings a sense of vocation to restore the provision and beauty and splendour of God's world.

It is not just a reverence for the creation and its creator which the discovery of God brings. It also brings a reverence for people, who are children of God. I find that some of the Old Testament betrays its primitive origins. To me it is anathema that God should devote whole cities to destruction: men, women and children, along with their sheep and cattle. It is anathema that people with deformities or serious handicap should be denied entry into the congregation of God, and that whole races should be regarded as beyond the love of God. Though I find so much strength, inspiration and wisdom in the Old Testament, there are times when I find it difficult to say or pray what is set down. I see it as the birth pangs of monotheism, and I believe that we have to make choices about what is written there. It bears so many signs of human projection onto God, and strays sometimes into portraying a sub-human God. It's therefore important to read the whole, to feast upon the light and wisdom it brings, but to recognize that it covers a two- or three-thousand-year voyage of discovering God, with many mistakes and traumas along the way. We need to learn more from the Jews as to how the Old Testament can be read and discerned. The Rabbis know some marvellous ways of interpreting the ancient word of God. In spite of some of the terrifying ideas of God, the seeds of the reverence for people are already powerfully sown in the Old Testament. Much of the understanding that we have is based there. In the prophets, the psalms, the wisdom literature, the struggling history of the people of Israel, in the journey of faith, and in the law of Moses, the vision of God is deep and broad and high, and Christians ignore it at their peril. Jesus as a Jew and a prophet stood firmly in the Jewish tradition, as did most of the first people who became Christian. He selected the two great commandments from the whole mass of the law; he set the love of our neighbour as the other great commandment to the love of God. The Ten Commandments remain wonderfully authoritative after nearly four millennia of the relatively short human history. In many ways, the reverence for people was already in waiting for the coming of Christ.

Although the Christian church has done many terrible things in its history, both on its own account and by its failure to prophesy to the nations, there is still no doubt that at the heart of the message of Jesus is reverence for people. It is so easy to take this remarkable fact for granted yet it is one of the most needed ingredients in our modern world. When I first discovered Jesus in a more personal way than the lessons I had been taught about him, it was this reverence for what each person had the capacity to be which thrilled me: his seeing through the scars and ulcerated limbs of the leper to a healed person; the generosity of spirit he saw in the prostitute who washed his feet with her tears; the walking man he saw in the bedridden cripple; the faith and honesty he saw in a soldier of the occupying forces; the sane and serene young man he perceived and discovered in the mentally crazy savage who tore himself with chains and screamed abuse at the world; the definitive good neighbour he held up for us all to see in a member of a despised race; the beauty he described in a wizened old woman who out of her poverty gave all that she had; the future companion in paradise whom he treasured, who hung beside him on a cross, who was to the crowds no more than the scum of the earth. So many examples make this one of the salient features of the Gospel at the centre of what it means to be holy. It's not a woolly left-wing do-gooder's invention; it is the vision of the Lord of life. It's a miracle that it has survived the terrible history of human brutality to fellow humans throughout history. It's a wonder that it hasn't been banned or burned out of existence.

Jesus did not only see the potential of the children of God in the defeated and despairing, the poor and the sinner; he also saw that potential in those whom he judged severely. The Kingdom of God was as near to each of them as the journey back to the loving father in Jesus' story of the prodigal son. Why did he so rage against the hypocritical religious? It was because they had twisted what was so precious. They knew about the justice which God required, they knew the law that God had given to his people, yet they turned it into bigotry, power and self-righteousness. He was threatening to the rich, because he knew their souls were often imprisoned by their concern for their wealth: trapped in their own values and priorities, failing even to see the poor beggar who lay desperate and full of sores at their very gate. He condemned their whitewash over sin, because it deceived people with a sham holiness. Even as he stood on trial before Pilate, Jesus understood the official's problem, his vacillation, and saw through to the person beneath the power who was condemning him to death.

It became clear to me that this was what Christ had done for me. He had seen through the mess that I was in my life, and in some ways still am. (As well as in ways I hadn't even thought of when I was 22!) 'Amazing grace that saved a wretch like me' was not a romantic overstatement by a hymn-writer but the simple truth of what I had discovered in finding God and discovering the love of Christ for me. But then it became urgent to discover this reverence for other people. It meant learning to get rid of so many of my attitudes. That parable Jesus told about the person forgiven his huge debts, who then went out into the world and made everyone pay up in full, became a judgement on me. How could I learn to see the child of God in everyone as Jesus had seen the child of God in me? I found individuals were often extremely unattractive, to put it mildly. There were types of people whom I despised. The battle goes on, and each age of a life brings the battle in new ways. Yet the failure to revere the potential of each person is what destroys so much in our world. Thank God we have much inside us that wants to love others, and we don't have to start from zero. It's just that the image of God in us is so corrupted and damaged by what happens to us and by our own wilful disobedience.

Look at the news each day and read the papers and keep your eyes and ears open, and you will see lack of reverence and respect all around you. Not just in the horrific wars but in the way drivers treat each other on the road, in the abuse of the referee on the local park football pitch, in the abuse of the old and the young, in the antics in the House of

Commons, in family relationships and in harassment at the workplace. It is obvious that this lies at the heart of so much conflict and suffering. It hardly needs saying, yet sometimes it feels as though we are going through some sort of soul barrier which is making it difficult for society to know when it is abusing its citizens and hard for individuals to see what Christ saw in others. His example and vision is so often lost behind easier and more readily available gods.

Jesus offers us a profoundly radical approach to life. It brings judgement as well as joy. It puts an end to being content to treat any category of human being as inferior to ourselves. It means seeing through the stereotypes to the real people each of us can be. Class distinction, racial and national prejudice, religious superiority become blind alleys. The old black woman sitting in the African village, living in a hut with nothing in it, surviving on the most basic food, is of the same value to God as the Lord Mayor of London or the Archbishop of Canterbury. The people queuing up for the dole, spending their days in the Jobcentres, or drinking themselves to oblivion on a park bench, are as valuable in the eyes of God as the managing director of a company earning half a million a year. The rent boy, the tart, the lonely person in the friendless zone, are as precious to Christ as the successful business man and jet-setter. The greatest Christians are those who have lived out this seemingly impossible creed of reverence for people and given the rest of us hope that it is not an impossible ideal but can be a practical reality in our own lives, if we find this Gospel for ourselves.

The movements to save the children, the refugees, the prisoners, the homeless exist in our society and we should not despair. Young and old people are attacked and raped, yet there is also great and loving care. For every dyed-in-the-wool racist, there is still an army of people who find their greatest satisfaction in the company and comradeship of other races. There is even a growing company of people who are finding each other across religious barriers. But these movements of the spirit need *you*. It's not just the dramatic acts of love and reconciliation between Catholic and Protestant in Northern Ireland, between brown and black, between rich and poor, but also the everyday relationships in our homes and at work that matter. How do we treat our wives/husbands? Do we show reverence for our parents/children? How do we respond to our neighbour?

When St Paul sets out to say what the Gospel requires of Christ's disciples, he uses this defining sentence: 'Be subject to one another out of reverence for Christ.' From this is derived the quality of all our relationships. It is to this the disciples are called. It is not far off in some unreachable place, but it is as near as the person next to you. It is our daily task. It is the way to find satisfaction. It's not about being a self-righteous or pious bore, or giving up the fun and beauty of life; it is to discover the fun and beauty in a richer way. It is often very hard, both heart- and back-breaking, but it is deeply rewarding. It expands what we hope we do for our own beloved people, our friends and our families, into a wider context of the brother- and sister-hood of all God's children. It is important too, that the holiest men and women are often the most abnormally normal people. They relish life given by God; humour is never far away. They have the ability to attend to you, though they may be severely pressed; they are free of pretence, and often can't abide false piety; and their lives bubble with the spring which comes from living close to the love of God. So often moral responsibility is portrayed as heavy duty; it does contain graft and tears, but it is also full of *joy*.

Anyone who follows Christ near enough to care in any way for the lost and the defeated knows that although what we do as individuals and groups is important, it can all be swept aside by politics, by national and international pressures. The picture comes to mind of the aid workers in Somalia, Rwanda, Bosnia or wherever. There we see them somehow coping with the impossible, with hundreds of thousands of refugees: binding up their wounds, providing food and clothing – only to be defeated by decisions made for political reasons, or because some leaders are afraid of losing power, or because the economy demands it. I'm not for a moment denying the difficulties of the political task. Indeed I believe that more people should consider taking part in politics. I am saying that, as well as the actions of individuals and groups, the Gospel has collective and national and international implications. It is important how we as individuals treat an immigrant, but it is so little if the law and the government treat them as less than human and can imprison or deport them without just cause. Justice is love in social terms, and it is just as important. If Archbishop Desmond Tutu and Nelson Mandela had simply been good individuals and prayed for the end of apartheid, it would have been part of the good; but it was necessary that they and their followers recognized that, to change the whole system, changes in the law were required as well as changes of heart.

Many of the younger generation care about these things and pursue them. Many hold strong opinions. They have received or developed for themselves a sense of moral responsibility from their own insights and experience, and from what has been handed down to them. But so much of this moral concern, derived in the past from the love of God and the sense of duty which the Christian conscience inspired, needed the strength given by faith to have the courage to act and to sustain the effort. Now it seems that many believe they don't need the 'God bit'. They seem to think that this stream flows on without the snow on the mountain tops, without the springs bubbling up from the Spirit of God, and therefore that they don't need prayer and they don't need any relationship with God. This I believe to be a profound and far-reaching error. It's almost as though we go on living off the spiritual capital of the past, without recognizing that it has to be constantly and daily renewed. I think there are many examples of this. Selfishness is a pervasive and powerful influence in us and it needs a strong challenge to divert it or even question it. Material gain is a seductive and persuasive power in our hearts and minds; we need a vision which springs from a spiritual critique, and sees possessions in proportion. Left to our nature, we seem hell-bent on acquisition and the spirit of giving is swallowed by the spirit of consuming. Even within our families, we can live off the spiritual capital as well as the material support. We all see the importance of the material capital but do we all see that the spiritual is even more important?

A Jewish taxi driver took me to Stepney once via Bethnal Green. He told me that his mother used to live in Bethnal

Green. He said that she was very religious. She observed the Sabbath to such an extent that she would rather go out into the street to ask someone to light the fire than break her own Sabbath rules. Her Jewish faith was the source of her strength by which she coped with an impossible life, and she gave him as a boy the security and love on which he had built his life. At one level he was saying that his mother went right over the top, but in another he was envious that she believed and prayed and worshipped Almighty God, and fed on the spiritual nourishment that he gave her. Now the taxi driver was a grandparent, and highly secularized. But he had begun to see there was something essential missing in his life. Though he had untold wealth compared with his mother, though he had a beautiful home, and a good job, there was something lacking and he was not at all sure how he was going to cope with everything life still had to throw at him. He was anxious because his children and their children were showing signs of losing the roots which had nourished him, and which he had taken in with his mother's milk. Perhaps it was just nostalgia for his mother and the 'good old days' but I felt it was much more than that. It was a recognition that much of the quality of their lives as children in the war, and before it, was built upon his mother's faith in God. Without that faith, the values, the moral strength seemed to have slowly ebbed away. I don't know whether he ever did anything about it but I know that in the conversation he articulated the loss in his life, which had come through thinking he could do it without the 'God bit'.

So many of the best attitudes in our society are built on Christian and faith foundations. Many people assume that the religion is simply part of the pool of human experience; they don't seem to realize that the pool becomes stagnant, silted up and leaks away. God is Spirit. God is living. Our living derives from God. He is not a thing of the past like a piece of Greek sculpture. God is a personal and direct fact of our lives now. It will not work if we think we can have the morality without the love of God, the refreshment of prayer, the study of God. The conscience which does not recognize God, which does not relate to God, is a conscience setting off on a different journey, and it may well reach a very different

destination. It can't be carried by someone else on our behalf
... well, not for long. Without the relationship with God,
who challenges our selfish and self-centred motivation? Who
sustains our best loving, not just of those we like, but of our
neighbour? Who enables us to go on forgiving and who frees
us by forgiving us? Who sustains us in goodness? What are
the streams of faith on which we are drawing and are they
going to dry up or be replenished? The examination of our
conscience is then a priority, because it cannot survive as a
vibrant Christian light without belief and trust in God in its
own day.

I have written this not from any sense of self-righteousness. As I get older I become more and more aware of
the failures and mess I have made of many things in my life. I
write rather out of the love which I feel for the younger
generation because I don't want them to lose sight of the
goodness, the beauty, the hope and the faith that can be
found in God. I find it impossible to contemplate how
generations to come will lead the best human life without
access to the love of God in a direct and personal way. It
frightens me to think of a society without the love and
example and critique of Jesus Christ. The conscience needs
the mind of Christ working in us. This fear of the loss of
Christ is a bit faithless on my part because, if God is God,
then he will always spring up anew in each generation. But
we do have the freedom to ignore and even reject him.

What are people basing their lives on who have no belief
in God? On their own opinions? Opinions are important but
they are an exceedingly narrow and frail basis for a life. When
the storms come, when there is only grief inside, when the
pressures and anxieties mount up, what is the source of
strength, hope and wisdom? When we are successful and all
seems right with us, and we are blind to the desperate needs
of our world, or turn our back on what we ought to do out
of our strength and good fortune – who calls our conscience
to account, who can penetrate our self-satisfaction? If it is all
based on our own opinions, it is our same unchallenged self
making the moral pace.

The Christian faith has stood the test of time; its ideas and
Christ's story have wonderfully developed and revealed new

understanding through two thousand years. Time after time it has looked as though it was going to fall but the holiness of Christ, the prophets and the faithful have prayed their way through. I am profoundly concerned that faith is being regarded as a sort of entertainment. The worship of God should never be boring but it is not primarily entertainment. We are in an age where entertainment looms large. It is a major industry. There always have to be bigger and more splendid feasts for the eyes and ears. There has to be noise and distraction rather than attention to the present moment with all its potential. In our day, the church is properly rediscovering that feelings and passion are important in the religious life and that the old ways had become, in the Church of England at least, rather dry and rationalistic. Now the bones are beginning to come to life and shake about and it is all the more important to test where we are going for truth and moral integrity. We need plenty of feeling in the head and plenty of thinking in the heart. When a person embraces the Christian faith, it is not just their own opinion, nor is it just the opinion of their congregation – however lively it may be – it is about learning the faith as taught by the church based upon the Bible, on the tradition of the church and upon reasoned and experienced thought. The age of individualism should not lead us to believe that it is just our own opinion or ideas which count; it is the faith presented afresh in each generation.

This concept of the teaching of the *Church* – not just of our vicar nor just of our lay leaders, but of the whole church – is an essential corrective to the congregational and individualistic version. This authority must never be a dead hand and we have to recognize that people need to explore what is new and exciting and can touch the heart. But there also need to be checks from something more tested and enduring and recognized by the church to be authentic. Every Christian should be their own theologian but the authority resides in the church not just in ourselves. This, too, is hard for new generations to accept, because, as I discussed earlier, authority has been under such heavy fire in all walks of life. Fashions change so quickly as we move from moment to moment. Every idea is expendable, and great and beautiful and essential ideas are so easily surrendered to the trite and the vague. The supermarket and the media bombardment provide such an abundance of choice and hype and propaganda which can be dazzling and bewildering. It's hard to find firm ground on which to base our faith. Fashion leads us by the nose if we let it. It appears to be a common response to imagine that we are our own main source of authority. Very soon this shallow source is found to be empty and it cannot stand up to the depth and violence and wickedness in the world, the barbarism which is never far from the human race. It will not stand the test. The weakness of will of the well-to-do is not deep enough to cope with reality.

This deficient understanding of authority is partly the result of education both in school and at home. We were rightly concerned to encourage children to work out their own opinions and make their own decisions. The two World Wars showed how dangerous authoritarian attitudes are. But, as so often, we see what needs to be changed but don't give sufficient care to the new we put in its place. There is a proper place for authority in the home and in the school. Without it the Lord of the Flies anarchy soon rules. The vacuum will soon be filled by various sorts of personal and corporate power. Without proper authority, the bullies rule and the weak are unprotected. When people see this anarchy, they long for someone strong to lead them out of their fear into a promised land. So the result can be authoritarian rule. There is a familiar hunger in this longing. When a thousand Moonie brides and grooms line up to be married, when the political leader offers dictatorship, when the church behaves in an absolutist way, there are many who will be seduced if they see anarchy as the only alternative. But the answer is proper authority, not no authority. Faith is not just a matter of individual opinion but first a response to God and then a developing understanding of the faith of the church. The right way to tackle the issue is to affirm the importance of people thinking things out for themselves but at the same time to recognize that there is need for a proper authority. If we ask a doctor's opinion, we may want a second opinion, or check out the advice given, but we also recognize that there is authority carried forward by the whole experience of medicine and science. As always, there is no absolute authority but a life without any authority to trust is resting on shaky foundations.

Those in the church who have tried through several decades to encourage the younger adults to share in the life of the church know just how difficult it is. There are so many interests and entertainments and ambitions to pursue and the church they know can seem so unwelcoming and have an average age well above par! The services can seem archaic and lacking in excitement, and the whole proceeding appear very passive. I know that I tried to find faith without belonging to the church but it doesn't work. We need to be with others who believe, to be encouraged by them and to pray with them. We need to be taught the faith and have opportunity to think it through and debate it and test what is on offer. It has been thrilling to see more young adults coming to learn and, through a range of groups and classes, begin to make the faith their own. It is amazing how a church can change and grow by the arrival of younger people who are committed and will give themselves to the community. As a bishop I have seen vicars reinvigorated, and congregations restored, because two or three young adults have begun to explore the love of God. The reason why there aren't many younger people in some churches is in part because they have chosen not to be there and make it what it could be if they were.

We are looking for people who are willing to ask themselves the question about God, who have realized what it means to live without the love of God and want to discover God for themselves. It requires originality, determination and a spirit of enquiry. I recently confirmed a young woman who in a short time had climbed to the top of her profession. She surprised herself by finding that her success had raised other questions to face and answer. As she said to the vicar when she knocked on his door, 'There must be more to life than this? What is it?' We often see that it is through the question in a person's mind that God rouses the person out of sleep and gives them a longing to know for themselves the love of God. This is why the conscience is such an important area of exploration. But the gate of heaven is not primarily about arguments and questions; though they have to be faced, the prime need is to discover prayer and action. The real and thorough search of the conscience will tell you if you are asleep where you ought to be alive. It can enable you to face the 'Thou' who is seeking for you in return. But it is through learning to pray and by a willingness to give service that we take the key steps. Some people are the sort of characters to whom prayer is the natural way to God; and there are others who find that loving action is the route to Him. Thankfully we are all different. Both prayer and action are needed, but our personality types will in part push us in one direction rather than another.

Whether by prayer, thought, word or deed, discovering God is the beginning of a new and profoundly exalting journey. It is to climb the mountain and find ourselves on holy ground. Once we've seen the view from the height, even if only for a moment, the desire to go on climbing, searching, struggling with the nights as well as the days, becomes irresistible. As we climb we realize that we do not climb alone but in the company of Jesus Christ through the strength of the Spirit. Happy climbing!